God as Father
and Priests as Fathers, Brothers, Bridegrooms, and Disciples

Fr. Peter Samuel Kucer, MSA

En Route Books and Media, LLC
Saint Louis, MO

En Route Books and Media, LLC
5705 Rhodes Avenue
St. Louis, MO 63109

Cover credit: TJ Burdick

ISBN-13: 978-0-9991143-9-1
Library of Congress Control Number:
2017956384

Copyright © 2017 Peter Samuel Kucer

All rights reserved.

Dedication

In memory of my mother, Roberta Kucer, who instilled in me a love of study and a love of her people, the chosen people.

In addition, I dedicate this book to the members of my community, the Missionaries of the Holy Apostles.

Acknowledgments

I would particularly like to acknowledge Fr. Isaac Martinez, MSA, former General of the Missionaries of the Holy Apostles, who gave me permission to publish, and Bishop Christian Rodembourg, MSA, who as the first MSA to be ordained a bishop brought our MSA charism into a deeper ecclesial dimension by assuming the office of bishop the year this book was published.

Special thanks to Dr. Sebastian Mahfood, OP, president of En Route Books and Media, for publishing this work.

Table of Contents

Preface v

Ch. 1 Father Gods & Rulers in Ancient Greece and Rome 1
   Gods and Rulers as Fathers in Ancient Greece ... 1
   Gods and Rulers as Fathers in Ancient Rome 6
   Chapter 1 Discussion Questions 13

Ch. 2 God as Father in the Old Testament 15
   God as a Non-Violent Creator 15
   God as Father in the Old Testament 20
   God as Father of Israel's Kings 24
   Chapter 2 Discussion Questions 26

Ch. 3 God the Father in the New Testament 29
   Visible Christian Community United by the
      Heavenly Father 30
   Distinctive Qualities of the Christian Father
      Centered Community 37
   Reasons for the Christian Father Centered
      Community 43
   Chapter 3 Discussion Questions 45

Ch. 4 Post-Apostolic and Post-Constantine Church 47
   Early Church of the Church Fathers and Early
      Christian Writers 47
   Post-Constantine Church 61

Chapter 4 Discussion Questions 71

Ch. 5 Priests as Fathers 73
    Fathers Who Harm and Atheism 74
    Fathers Who Heal 78
    Chapter 5 Discussion Questions 90

Ch. 6 Priests as Brothers 91
    Priests as Signs of Heavenly Fraternity 91
    Priestly Fraternity 98
    Chapter 6 Discussion Questions 106

Ch. 7 Divine Love in Paganism 109
    Divine Love in Mythology 109
    Love in Greek Philosophy 115
    Chapter 7 Discussion Questions 120

Ch. 8 God as Bridegroom & Israel as Bride 121
    Created Out of Love 121
    Chosen by God Out of Love 127
    Israel's Marital Obligations 131
    Chapter 8 Discussion Questions 132

Ch. 9 Jesus as Bridegroom & the Church as Bride . 135
    Wedding at Cana 136
    Samaritan Woman 137
    Eucharist 139
    The Passion, Crucifixion, Resurrection and
        Second Coming 142
    Christian Marriage 145

Chapter 9 Discussion Questions 149

Ch. 10 Early Church and Magisterium on Marriage 151
    Early Church on Marriage 151
    Magisterial Teaching on Marriage....................... 159
    Chapter 10 Discussion Questions 168

Chapter 11 Priests as Bridegrooms 171
    The Glory of the Priesthood 172
    The Cross of the Priesthood 178
    Chapter 11 Discussion Questions 183

Chapter 12 Priests as Disciples of Jesus 185
    Church Men 187
    Disciples of Christ 192
    Chapter 12 Discussion Questions 198

Preface

The vocation to the priesthood does not simply entail doing specific actions that only priests can perform. Being a priest essentially means being grounded in the unique identity of participating in the headship of Christ. More specifically, this means priests are to understand themselves in a relational way, including as fathers, brothers, bridegrooms, and disciples.

In this work, we will reflect on this personal understanding of the priesthood in two parts, first, by reflecting on the mystery of the priesthood from the perspective of father, and then by reflecting on the priesthood from the viewpoint of bridegroom. In these sections, what Revelation teaches us regarding priests as fathers, brothers, bridegrooms and disciples will be presented and clarified by Catholic wisdom throughout the ages, including from modern times. In addition, the historical contexts in which these terms were first used in Revelation and the Church will also be touched upon to better understand the unique Christian difference.

Chapter 1

Father Gods and Rulers in Ancient Greece and Rome

Introduction

We will begin our study with how the ancient Greeks and Romans understood fatherhood in their mythology and how they conceived of fatherhood with respect to their country and rulers. The subsequent two chapters will then contrast the Greek and Roman concept of Fatherhood with the biblical understanding of God as Father. First, we will focus on the Greek concept before reflecting on the Roman understanding.

Gods and Rulers as Fathers in Ancient Greece

According to Homer, all the gods acknowledged Zeus as their Father. Book II of the *Iliad* reads, "All the gods together rose from their seats before the face of their father [Zeus]; no one dared to await his coming, but they all rose up before him."[1]

---

[1] Homer, "Homer, *Iliad*, Book 1, line 531," perseus.tufts.edu, http://www.perseus.tufts.edu/hopper/text?doc=Perseus%3Atext%3A1999.01.0134%3Abook%3D1%

His omnipotent power is evident in his control over thunder and lightning and appearance as a powerful bull before he seduced the woman Europa, one of many women Zeus seduced. The history of this father of the gods is quite relevant, as we will see later. Zeus was the youngest child of the Titan Cronus who ate his children upon their birth. Rhea, Zeus' mother, saved Zeus from being devoured by his father, who ate his children to prevent them from challenging his rule.

Rhea tricked her husband, handing him a clothed rock which he thought was his son Zeus. When Zeus had grown strong enough to challenge his father, he allied himself with the goddess Metis, who gave Cronus a drink that caused him to vomit out all his children he had eaten. With gratitude to their younger brother, these liberated gods successfully overthrew Cronus. Afterwards, Zeus became the god of the heavens and king of all the gods. In imitation of his father's fear of being challenged by his children, though, Zeus ate Metis who was pregnant with his son.[2]

3Acard%3D531. The citation is as follows. Homer. The Iliad with an English Translation by A.T. Murray, Ph.D. in two volumes. Cambridge, MA., Harvard University Press; London, William Heinemann, Ltd. 1924.

[2] Edith Hamilton, *Mythology* (New York: Little, Brown and Company, 1976), 17, 20, 79, 103. Kathleen N. Daly,

Notice the recurring theme of violent rivalry between sons and fathers in Greek mythology. Even Cronus's father, Uranus, saw his children as rivals and, for that reason, imprisoned his children, including Cronus, deep in earth, in other words deep in the earth goddess, Gaia. Gaia, in pain in having her children thrust inside of her, gave Cronus a knife to use against his father. In attacking his father, Cronus castrated him and then threw his father's testicles into the sea.[3]

In *The Odyssey*, Homer, through the character Philoetius, describes Zeus as a violent, uncaring, wrathful father who is greatly feared. He writes, "Father Jove [Zeus], of all gods you are the most malicious. We are your own children, yet you show us no mercy in all our misery and afflictions."[4] This despotic understanding of Zeus as the principal father influenced how Greeks understood fatherhood among men. As the Greek Stoic Epictetus explains, quoting a poet, "I must not, even if a worse man than you should come, treat a father unworthily, for all are

---

Greek and Roman Mythology A to Z, Third Edition (New York: Chelsea House Publishers, 2009), 92.

[3] Hesiod, "The Theogony of Hesiod, translated by Hugh G. Evelyn-White, 1914," II, 116-206, sacred-texts.com, http://www.sacred-texts.com/cla/hesiod/ theogony.htm

[4] Homer, "The Odyssey," Book XX, classics.mit.edu, http://classics.mit.edu/Homer/odyssey.20.xx.html

from paternal Zeus."[5] In his advice to sons Epictetus (C. 55-135 AD) emphasizes the despotic character of fathers, traceable to Zeus:

> After this, remember that you are a son. What does this character promise? To consider that everything which is the son's belongs to the father, to obey him in all things, never to blame him to another, nor to say or do anything which does him injury, to yield to him in all things and give way, cooperating with him as far as you can.[6]

Earlier, Aristotle (384-322 BC) likewise traced a father's role back to Zeus' despotic kingship. In book one of his *Politics*, he associates fatherhood with monarchy, but in respect to his children and not to his wife. He writes, "The rule of a household is a monarchy, for every house is under one head: whereas constitutional rule is a government of freemen and equals."[7] A few sections later, Aristotle further ex-

---

[5] Epictesus, "The Discourses," Book 3, Chapter 11, http://classics.mit.edu/Epictetus/discourses.3.three.html

[6] Epictesus, "The Discourses," Book 2, Chapter 10, http://classics.mit.edu/Epictetus/discourses.2.two.html; Gerhard Kittel and Gerhard Friedrich, *The Theological Dictionary of the New Testament* (Grand Rapids: Wm. B. Eerdmans Publishing Company, 1964), Strong's Greek #3962.

[7] Gerhard Kittel and Gerhard Friedrich, *The Theological Dictionary of the New Testament* (Grand Rapids: Wm. B. Eerdmans Publishing Company, 1964), Strong's Greek

plains that with respect to his children a father is to rule as a monarch. However, with respect to his wife a father is to rule with "constitutional rule."[8]

#3962; Aristotle, "Politics" book 1, part VII, http://classics.mit.edu/Aristotle/politics.1.one.html

[8] Gerhard Kittel and Gerhard Friedrich, *The Theological Dictionary of the New Testament* (Grand Rapids: Wm. B. Eerdmans Publishing Company, 1964), Strong's Greek #3962; Aristotle, "Politics" book 1, part XII, http://classics.mit.edu/Aristotle/politics.1.one.html. "Of household management we have seen that there are three parts- one is the rule of a master over slaves, which has been discussed already, another of a father, and the third of a husband. A husband and father, we saw, rules over wife and children, both free, but the rule differs, the rule over his children being a royal, over his wife a constitutional rule. For although there may be exceptions to the order of nature, the male is by nature fitter for command than the female, just as the elder and full-grown is superior to the younger and more immature. But in most constitutional states the citizens rule and are ruled by turns, for the idea of a constitutional state implies that the natures of the citizens are equal, and do not differ at all. Nevertheless, when one rules and the other is ruled we endeavor to create a difference of outward forms and names and titles of respect, which may be illustrated by the saying of Amasis about his foot-pan. The relation of the male to the female is of this kind, but there the inequality is permanent. The rule of a father over his children is royal, for he rules by virtue both of love and of the respect due to age, exercising a kind of royal power. And therefore Homer has ap-

Gods and Rulers as Fathers in Ancient Rome

The Romans identified many of their gods with gods of the Greeks. For example, the Greek god Zeus was identified by the Romans as Jupiter (also known as Jove). Although, like the Greeks, Romans considered Jupiter their principal god, they also were especially devoted to Mars, the god of war. This devotion to Mars provides a contrast with a central city state of the Greeks, Athens, whose chief goddess was Athena, goddess of reason and daughter of Zeus. In Roman Mythology, Mars, by raping the vestal virgin Rhea Silvia, fathered two twin sons: Romulus and Remus.[9] After giving birth to the twins, Rhea abandoned them by placing them in a vessel on the Tiber river. Upon being washed up on shore, the twins were adopted by a she-wolf. When they grew up, the twins left the she-wolf and set out on their own. Working together, the two brothers founded a city. Tension, though, arose between them, causing Romulus to murder his brother Remus. Romulus then named the city after himself, which, according to legend is the origin of the word

---

propriately called Zeus 'father of Gods and men,' because he is the king of them all. For a king is the natural superior of his subjects, but he should be of the same kin or kind with them, and such is the relation of elder and younger, of father and son."

[9] Cheryl Perry, *Mythology: Myths, Legends, & Fantasies* (Cape Town: Struik Publishers, 2006), 203.

Rome.[10]

Romulus, who reflected the terrifying father-hood of Zeus, was revered by the Romans. According to the ancient Roman writer Quintus Ennius (c. 239-169 BC), there was even a practice among the Romans when grieving for a recently deceased king to honor him by comparing him to Romulus with the words, "O Romulus, godly Romulus, what a guardian of your country did the gods beget you! O father and begetter, O blood sprung from the god!' *They used to call those whom they had lawfully obeyed not lords and masters, nor yet again kings, but guardians of their country, yes and fathers and gods. Nor was this without reason. For what do they say next?* - You it was who brought us forth into the world of light."[11]

A particularly famous legendary ancestor of Rom-

---

[10] C. Scott Littleton, *Gods, Goddesses, and Mythology*, Volume 6 (New York: Marshall Cavendish, 2005), 835; "Titus Livius (Livy), *The History of Rome*, Books 4-7, trans. Benjamin Oliver Foster, Perseus, http://www.perseus.tufts.edu/hopper/text?doc=Perseus%3Atext%3A1999.02.0151%3Abook%3D1%3Achapter%3D4; Thomas F.X. Noble, *The Foundations of Western Civilization*, Lectures 1-24 (Chantilly: The Great Courses, 2002), 242-282.

[11] Ennius, "Ennius: Annales (fragments)," book II, 117-20, http://www.attalus.org/poetry/ennius1.html; Abera M. Mengestu, *God as Father in Paul* (Eugene: Pickwick Publications, 2013), 59.

ulus, Aeneas,[12] likewise founded a city after murdering his rival. The city Aeneas founded, Lavinium, preceded and, in mythology, prepared for Rome's founding.[13] Aeneas was supposedly the son of the goddess Aphrodite (Venus for the Romans) and cousin of the king of Troy, King Priam. After Troy fell during the Trojan War, Aeneas fled with his father, Anchises, representing tradition, on his back to Italian lands. There, he engaged in battle and upon successfully defeating his rival Turnus he founded the city of Lavinium. Despite his father's counsel that he is "to spare the humbled foe,"[14] Aeneas kills Turnus while Turnus lays subdued at his feet. As described by Virgil, standing over Turnus Aeneas "with kindling rage and terrifying look…buried deep his furious blade in the opposer's [Turnus's] heart…."[15]

The Roman association of their founding fathers,

---

[12] According to Virgil's *Aeneid*, Aeneas is related to Romulus and Remus. See *Aeneid*, book 1, 254-297.

[13] Ibid.

[14] Virgil, "Aeneid," book 6, lines 801ff, http://www.perseus.tufts.edu/hopper/text?doc=Perseus%3Atext%3A1999.02.0054%3Abook%3D6%3Acard%3D801. The citation given is as follows. Vergil. Aeneid. Theodore C. Williams. trans. Boston. Houghton Mifflin Co. 1910.

[15] Virgil, "Aeneid," book 12, verse 919 ff, http://www.perseus.tufts.edu/hopper/text?doc=Perseus%3Atext%3A1999.02.0054%3Abook%3D12%3Acard%3D919.

both gods and men, with violence became reflected in how they perceived the relationship of fathers in families. Like the Greeks, the Romans typically held that the Father is the head of his household. This headship even included the legal right, sometimes called *jus vitae necisque*, to treat his children as slaves and even to punish his children by killing them.[16] Not until the Christian Emperor Justinian (482-565 AD) was this and similar laws put aside.[17] The Roman ju-

---

[16] In referring to this law the Roman jurist Gaius (130-180 AD) writes, "But, as among Roman citizens, a double ownership may exist (for a slave is understood to be subject to bonitarian or quiritarian right or to belong to both these classes) so we merely say that a slave is in the power of his owner if he forms part of his property by bonitarian right, even if at the same time he may not belong to him by quiritarian right; for anyone who has the bare quiritarian right in a slave is not understood to have him in his power. This right is peculiar to Roman citizens, for there are hardly any other men who have such authority over their children as we have, and this the Divine Hadrian stated in the Edict which he published with reference to persons who petitioned for Roman citizenship for themselves and for their children...." Gaius, "The Institutes of Gaius: The Four Commentaries of Gaius on the Institutes of the Civil Law," no. 54-55, http://www.constitution.org/sps/sps01_2-1.htm.

[17] Gerhard Kittel and Gerhard Friedrich, *The Theological Dictionary of the New Testament*, electronic ed., Vol. 5, (Grand Rapids: Wm. B. Eerdmans Publishing Company, 1964), 950.

rist Ulpian (c. 170-223 AD) defined this mythologically influenced understanding of a father of a family as one who stands outside and over the family, which is to submit to his hierarchical power.[18]

---

[18] Charles J. Reid, *Power Over the Body, Equality in the Family: Rights and Domestic Relations* (Grand Rapids: Wm. B. Eerdmans Publishing Co, 2004), 71-72. In Justinian's *Digest* an excerpt from Ulpian reads, "195. *The Same, On the Edict, Book XLVI.*

The term "masculine" frequently extends to both sexes.

(1) Let us see how the word "family" should be understood. And indeed, it is understood in various ways, for it has reference to both property and persons; to property, as in the Law of the Twelve Tables where it is said, "Let the next of kin on the father's side have the estate" *(familia)*. The term "family" also has reference to persons, as where the same law referring to a patron and his freedman says, "From this family to that." In this instance, it is established that the law has reference to individuals.

(2) The term "family" has reference to every collection of persons which are connected by their own rights as individuals, or by the common bond of general relationship. We say that a family is connected by its own rights where several are either by nature or by law subjected to the authority of one; for example, the father of a family, the mother of a family, and a son and a daughter under paternal control, as well as their descendants; for instance, grandsons, granddaughters, and their successors. He is designated the father of a family who has authority over the household, and he is properly so called even if he has

no son, for we do not merely consider his person, but also his right. Then we also style a minor the father of a family, when his father dies, and each of the persons who were under his control begins to have a separate household, and all obtain the title of father of a family. The same thing happens in the case of a son who is emancipated, for he also has his own family when he becomes independent. We say that the family of all the agnates is a common one, because even though the head of the household may be dead, and each of them has a separate family, still, all who were under the control of him alone are properly said to belong to the same family, as they have sprung from the same house and race.

(3) We are also accustomed to apply the term "family" to bodies of slaves, as we explained, according to the Edict of the Praetor, under the Title of Theft, where the Praetor mentions the family of farmers of the revenue. In this instance, all slaves are not meant, but only those are designated who were appointed for this purpose, that is to say, for the collection of taxes. In another part of the Edict all slaves are included; as in the case of unlawful assemblies, and property taken by force, and also where suit for the annulment of a contract can be brought, and the property is returned in a worse condition through the act of the purchaser or his family; and finally, in the case of the interdict *Unde vi,* the term family embraces not only all the slaves, but also the children.

(4) The word "family" also applies to all those persons, who are descended from the last father, as we say the Julian Family, referring, as it were, to persons derived from a certain origin within our memory.

In time, Roman rulers also perceived their role as fathers who stand outside and over their subjects. This Roman cult of the ruler was influenced by the earlier history of the ancient Egyptian Pharaohs who were worshipped as sons of gods.[19] Capitalizing on this connection, Julius Caesar (100-44 BC) claimed that not only was he a descendant of Aeneas, but he

---

(5) The wife is the beginning and the end of her family." "The Enactments of Justinian: The Digest or Pandects," Book L, 16, http://droitromain.upmf-grenoble.fr/Anglica/D50_Scott.htm#XVI.

[19] Gerhard Kittel and Gerhard Friedrich, *The Theological Dictionary of the New Testament*, electronic ed., vol. 5, (Grand Rapids: Wm. B. Eerdmans Publishing Company, 1964), 952; A very early reference to Pharaoh's as a son of God is from Utterance 571 of the Ancient Egyptian Pyramid texts: "O you who die not because of a king, this King will not die because of a king; O! you who die not because of any dead, the King will not die because of any dead, for the King is an Imperishable Star, son of the sky-goddess who dwells in the Mansion of Selket. Ra has taken this King to himself to the sky so that this King may live, just as he who enters into the west of the sky lives when he goes up in the east of the sky…" R.O. Faulkner, *The Ancient Egyptian Pyramid Texts* (Stilwell: Digireads.com Publishing, 2007), 226-227. These texts date 2000 years before the birth of Christ. James P. Allen, *The Ancient Egyptian Pyramid Texts* (Atlanta: Society of Biblical Literature, 2005), 1.

also was a descendant of Venus, goddess of fertility.[20] Later, his grand-nephew and adopted son, Gaius Octavius (63 BC-14 AD), later named Augustus, explicitly called himself a son of god with the title *Imperator Caesar Divi Filius*.[21] Another title Augustus promoted was *Pontifex Maximus*, signifying that not only was he Rome's first emperor but also was Rome's high priest. As Rome's first Emperor, Augustus promoted himself as the father of the fatherland with the term *pater patria*. In his view, he was an absolute father who stood over his people, his children and provided them with the peaceful security of his *Pax Romana*.[22]

Chapter 1 Discussion Questions

1. Chronologically describe the violent characteristics and rivalrous nature of the fathers of the Greek gods. Include the following in your response: Uranus, Gaia, Cronus, Rhea, Zeus, and Metis.

---

[20] Abera M. Mengestu, *God as Father in Paul* (Eugene: Pickwick Publications, 2013), 32. Mengestu cites Seutonius, *Divus Julius*, 6.1.

[21] Michael Koortbojian, *The Divinization of Caesar and Augustus* (New York: Cambridge University Press, 2013), 11-12, 145, 165.

[22] Mengestu, *God as Father in Paul*, 63, 68.

2. According to the chapter, how was the Greek concept of fatherhood influenced by Greek mythology? Include the following in your response: Despot, Epictetus, Aristotle, children, and obedience.

3. Describe the violent characteristics and rivalrous nature of the Roman god Mars in relationship to the human fathers, mythological and actual, of ancient Rome. Include the following in your answer: Mars, Aeneas, Rhea Silvia, Romulus, Remus, Rome, *jus vitae necisque*, Julius Caesar, and Augustus.

Chapter 2

God as Father in the Old Testament

Introduction

The Old Testament also identifies God as a father but in a very different way from how the Greeks and Romans understood fatherhood among their gods. We will examine these differences in the following ways: first, God as a non-violent creator, second, God as loving, merciful Father, and third, God as Father of Israel's kings and of individuals.

God as a Non-Violent Creator

As is evident in the previous chapter, in Greek and Roman mythology divine fatherhood was associated with violence. The one who wielded the power of father of the other gods used his power to crush, dominate and even eliminate his own children. At times, the humiliated children revolt against their father to overthrow him, and this pattern is repeated by the children of the god who becomes the father of all.

With respect to God as presented in the Old Testament, points out Silke-Maria Weineck, both the killing of the father god and the killing of children by the father god is absent.[1] In addition, the creation of the world is not presented as the byproduct of a war between gods who fought to determine who will rule the other and in which the scattered remains of the defeated gods become the various parts of the universe. In other words, a Catholic understanding of creation rejects the idea that the universe was created out of pre-existing matter (*creatio ex materia*).

Instead, the Old Testament reveals a God who, as existence itself, as being itself, as the one who is not dependent on anything, including chaos or another god who fathered him, created the universe out of nothing (*creatio ex nihilo*). This teaching of the Catholic Church[2] is explicitly stated in 2 Maccabees, which states, "I beg you, my child, to look at the heaven and the earth and see everything that is in them, and recognize that God did not make them out of things that existed. And in the same way the human race came into being." (2 Maccabees 7:28 NRSV)

In traditional interpretation, the doctrine of creation out of nothing is implied in the first verse of Genesis, "In the beginning when God created the heavens and the

---

[1] Silke-Maria Weineck, *The Tragedy of Fatherhood: King Laius and the Politics of Paternity in the West* (New York: Bloomsbury, 2014), 40-41.

[2] "We believe that God needs no pre-existent thing or any help in order to create, nor is creation any wort of necessary emanation from the divine substance. God creates freely 'out of nothing.'" Catechism of the Catholic Church," no. 296, vatican.va, http://www.vatican.va/archive/ccc_css/archive/catechism/p1s2c1p4.htm. The following is referenced. *Dei Filius*, can. 2-4; DS 3022-3024, Lateran Council IV (1215): DC 800; cf. DS 3025.

earth, the earth was a formless void and darkness covered the face of the deep, while a wind from God swept over the face of the waters. Then God said, 'Let there be light'; and there was light. ... (Genesis 1:1-3 NRSV)

The words that Genesis uses, "Let there be" to describe God calling creation into existence out of nothing, comments Bishop Barron, are "a sheerly nonviolent, non-intrusive, non-interruptive act of speech."[3] Barron additionally explains that the teaching on creation out of nothing not only essentially differs from pagan origin myths but also greatly differs from "the more refined philosophical accounts of Plato and Aristotle, [where] the universe is formed through the imposition of form on recalcitrant matter."[4] In contrast, in the biblical account, writes Barron, "God does not wrestle a rival into submission, for he has no rival; nor does he intervene to shape matter according to his aggressive will, for there is no matter that confronts him."[5]

In Exodus 3:14, God reveals himself to Moses as existence itself, and, therefore, not a being among beings, a father among fathers. God simply reveals his identity to Moses with, "I am who I am." (Exodus 3:14 NRSV) We along with all of creation, in stark contrast with God, only exist because we participate in existence. We have existence, because God is existence. This means, as explained by Barron, that the God of Revelation is not a God who is in competition with what he has created but rather, espe-

---

[3] Robert Barron, *Catholicism: A Journey to the Heart of the Faith* (New York: Image Books, 2011) loc. 1069.

[4] Ibid.

[5] Ibid.

cially with respect to man, is a God who wants creation to more fully participate in His being in which all creation shares in.[6] For this reason, the bush through which God reveals himself to Moses is not consumed but rather becomes transformed and ennobled. The desire of God that all of creation will one day become like the burning bush will be fulfilled, promises Scripture, in the promised New Heavens and New Earth. (Revelation 21:1)

In describing the sustaining (*creatio continua*), non-competitive relationship God has with the world, Barron first points to Wisdom 8:1. Here, God's providential wisdom is depicted as ordering "all things sweetly." (Wisdom 8:1 DRA)[7] God revealed his gentle, sweet, sustaining pow-

---

[6] Robert Barron, *Catholicism: The New Evangelization*, DVDs (Word on Fire).

[7] Barron, *Catholicism*, loc. 1085-1092. "God's creativity and providence are necessarily expressions of the divine love and hence of the "letting be" of the other. The providential God is not one great cause among many, interfering with the nexus of conditioned causes. We recall the language of the book of Wisdom, how "sweetly" God exercises his power, operating precisely *through* the realm of secondary causes. Perhaps I could illustrate this with a simple example. If asked, 'How do you make a cherry pie,' one would say, presumably, 'you bring together cherries, sugar, flour, water, fat, and the skill of the baker, and the heat of the oven.' Even the religious believer would not say, 'You bring together cherries, sugar, flour, God, water, fat, and the skill of the baker and the heat of the oven.' God is not one cause among many, but rather the reason there are cherries, flour, water, fat, the baker, and so on, at

er to the prophet Elijah when He tells Elijah to "Go out and stand on the mountain before the Lord, for the Lord is about to pass by." (1 Kings 19:11 NRSV) A destructive wind that split apart rocks, an earthquake, and a fire all successively occurred before Elijah, but God did not reveal his presence to Elijah in any of these seemingly most powerful forces of nature. Rather, God revealed His presence in "sheer silence" (1 Kings 19:12 NRSV), also translated as "a gentle blowing" (NAB).

Because God is not a violent being in competition with lesser beings and with beings who are similarly powerful, He rejects, as contrary to the worship of His nature, any violent expressions of worship that were common among pagan religions, specifically the sacrifice of their children (*filicide*). In Genesis 22, God forbids Abraham from sacrificing his son to Him.[8] Such an act would be directly contrary to his nature as not only the Creator but also a loving father who creates to provide a suitable, caring home in which he placed his adopted children to live. Psalm 104 and Job 38-40, points out Scott Hahn, even "describe Creation as having a foundation, a cornerstone, a roof, doors, windows and other architectural features"[9]

---

all. Hence, it is precisely through those causes and not in competition with them that the providential God works out his purposes."

[8] Silke-Maria Weineck, *The Tragedy of Fatherhood: King Laius and the Politics of Paternity in the West* (New York: Bloomsbury, 2014), 40-41.

[9] Scott Hahn, *A Father Who Keeps His Promises: God's Covenant Love in Scripture* (Cincinnati: St. Anthony Messenger Press, 1998), 45.

precisely to teach that this world is not intended to be a place where life is, as Thomas Hobbes writes, "solitary, poor, nasty, brutish and short."[10]

The rooms of the first floor of this house, Hahn designates, with specific reference to Genesis 1:1-3 and Genesis 2:1-3, as day 1, day 2, and day 3 in which the formlessness becomes transformed into realms, respectively day and night, sea and sky, land and vegetation. Similarly, Hahn designates the second floor of the house as day 4, day 5, and day 6 in which the emptiness of the established "realms" are filled with "rulers" specifically sun and moon and stars, birds and fish, man and animals. The roof of the house, day seven, Hahn designates as the Sabbath, the day of rest, communion with God towards which all of creation is geared.[11]

God as Father in the Old Testament

Deuteronomy 32 identifies God as Father with "Is he not your father, who created you, who made you and established you?" (Deuteronomy 32:6 NRSV) Here, God's children are specifically the Israelites, for whom God cares as a faithful loving God even when his children act degenerately, perversely, crookedly, or foolishly. (Deuteronomy 32: 5-6). The Pentateuch's description of God as a faithful, loving father is particularly stressed, Abera M. Mengestu

---

[10] Thomas Hobbes, The Leviathan, (St. Paul's Churchyard: Green Dragon, 1651), chapter xiii, Project Gutenberg, "Leviathan by Thomas Hobbes," http://gutenberg.org/files/3207/3207-h/3207-h.htm.

[11] Hahn, *A Father Who Keeps His Promises*, 43.

points out, in prophetic literature. (Isaiah 63:16; 64:9; Jer. 3:4-5, 19; 31:9; Mal. 1:6, 2:10)[12]

Why God is consistently faithful to his children is explained in the Old Testament under the aspect of covenant. Unlike a contract, which is horizontally established between two equal parties, a covenant, at the time of Israelites, was an agreement vertically established between two unequal parties, such as between a King and a nation. In the Old Testament times, this both pagan and Israelite concept of covenant is presented in Revelation as an agreement between God and Israel.[13] Included in this covenant is a moral code that if broken requires punishing the violators and/or the fulfillment of purification rites not so much as a deterrent for further violations to the community, but rather so that God will not punish his people for breaking the punishment. Reflecting this Israelite understanding of their covenant with God, Deuteronomy 21 reads, "Absolve, O Lord, your people Israel, whom you have ransomed, and let not the guilt of shedding innocent blood remain in the midst of your people Israel." (Deuteronomy 21:8 NAB) These words are preceded by a purification rite for an "untraced murder."[14]

The reason why this vertical covenant agreement between God and Israel was, explains Joseph Ratzinger, "continually deepened and surpassed" specifically in the Old Testament prophetic literature is because "the cove-

---

[12] Abera M. Mengestu, *God as Father in Paul* (Eugene: Pickwick Publications, 2013), 105.

[13] Anthony Phillips, *Ancient Israel's Criminal Law* (New York: Schocken Books, 1970), 3-4.

[14] Phillips, *Ancient Israel's Criminal Law*, 12.

nant relation of Yahweh to Israel is a covenant of marital love, which—as in Hosea's magnificent vision—moves and stirs Yahweh himself to his heart."[15]

This transformed and elevated covenant relationship that Israel has with God is not simply one between a superior and subordinate, but, in addition, between the loving Father, God, and his children, the Israelites. These covenanted Israelites, explains Hahn, were not elected for their own sake but for the sake of others, so that all may one day become members of a universal, worldwide family.[16]

---

[15] Joseph Ratzinger, *Daughter Zion: Meditations on the Church's Marian Belief*, trans. McDermott (San Francisco: Ignatius Press, 1983), 21-22.

[16] "From the beginning, his desire was to father a worldwide family. He singled out Abraham, Isaac, Jacob and Moses, not because he plays favorites but because he is a wise father who knows how to use his firstborn son to influence the younger siblings who have been deceived by demonic powers. God allowed the Davidic kings to make vassals out of the surrounding nations for their own good. After all, it was better to serve as a slave in God's family than to be free outside of his household." Scott Hahn, *A Father Who Keeps His Promises: God's Covenant Love in Scripture* (Cincinnati: St. Anthony Messenger Press, 1998), 214. The following covenant chart that follows Hahn's account is based on the following source. Sarah Christmyer, *A Quick Journey Through the Bible: An 8-Part Introduction to the Bible Timeline Student Workbook* (West Chester: Ascension Press, 2008), 12.

(As we will see in a subsequent chapter, this is fulfilled in the Catholic Church.)

With reference to Karl Barth, Hans Urs von Balthasar explains that Israel's chosen status and the later chosen status of the predominately Gentile Church complemented one another so that all, Gentile and Jew, would, through Jesus Christ, become members of God's family. The Israelites were first chosen and then rejected for the sake of others, specifically the Gentiles. In turn, and as a mirror complementary image, the Gentiles were rejected and then chosen for the sake of Israel.[17]

Family Form	Mediator	Covenant Sign
One Holy Couple	Adam (Gen 1-3)	Sabbath
One Holy Family	Noah (Gen 9)	Rainbow
One Holy Tribe	Abraham (Gen 15, 17,22)	Circumcision
One Holy Nation	Moses (Ex 24/ Deut 29)	Tablets
One Holy Kingdom	David/Solomon (II Sam. 7)	Ark and Tent/ Temple
One Holy Catholic Church	Jesus (Mk 14)	Eucharist

[17] Han Urs von Balthasar, *The Theology of Karl Barth*, trans. Edward T. Oakes (San Francisco: Ignatius Press,

God as Father of Israel's Kings

Not only was Israel considered God's favored people, his favored children, for the sake of other peoples, but also their Davidic king is referred to in the Old Testament as a son of God. In 2 Samuel 7, we read, "…the Lord came to Nathan: Go and tell my servant David: … the Lord will make you a house. … I will be a father to him, and he shall be a son to me." (2 Samuel 7:4, 11, 14 NRSV) David is considered a son of the Lord not in the sense of being quasi-divine as Alexander the Great, Julius Caesar, and Caesar Augustus all claimed to be.

Unlike these and other great kings from ancient times, no king of Israel was ever worshiped. Instead, their kingship, explains Abba Hillel Silver, was understood in a more "democratic" sense as personifying the kingship of all the people. Reflecting this belief, Exodus 19 states, "You shall be a kingdom of priests." (Exodus 19:6 NAB) This participatory manner of understanding kingship is also reflected in that the Sinai covenant was made with "all the men of Israel" (Deuteronomy 29:9 NAB) and in Moses's desire that "all the people of the Lord were prophets."[18] (Numbers 11:29 NAB)

Silver also contrasts Israel's kings with other kings from the ancient world by pointing out that unlike the absolute rule so common among Egyptian pharaohs and Asi-

---

1992), loc. 3760. Balthasar refers to Barth's exegesis of Romans 9-11.

[18] Abba Hillel Silver, *Where Judaism Differs: An Inquiry into the Distinctiveness of Judaism* (New York: Collier Books, 1989), 234.

atic kings, in which the kings where exempt from the moral law governing their kingdoms, kings of Israel are presented in the bible as accountable to moral law along with everyone else. For this reason, the prophets freely denounced kings when they violated moral law, notably Samuel with Saul, Nathan with David, Shemaiah with Rehoboam, Jehu with Baasa, Elijah with Ahab, and Jeremiah with Zedekiah.[19]

This Jewish understanding of their kings in a fraternal manner as one of the people is also evident in that not only were Davidic kings understood as God's sons but, as the book of Sirach indicates, an individual Jew may also address God as his father not only in a collective sense but also in a personal, individual sense. In Sirach 23, we read, "Lord, Father and Master of my life, permit me not to fall by them. ... Lord, Father and God of my life, abandon me not into their control." (Sirach 23: 1, 4 NAB) Similarly, Sirach 51:10 states, "I called out: O Lord, you are my father, you are my champion and my savior...." (Sirach 51:10 NAB)[20]

Around the time of Jesus, the Hellenic Jewish philosopher Philo of Alexandria (c. 25 BC-50 AD) helped to further expand and develop the Jewish understanding of God's fatherhood as extending above and including all people as his children, who are to be brothers and sisters

---

[19] Abba Hillel Silver, *Where Judaism Differs: An Inquiry into the Distinctiveness of Judaism* (New York: Collier Books, 1989), 237. 1 Samuel 15; 2 Samuel 12; 2 Chronicles 11: 2-4; 1 Kings 16: 1-4; 1 Kings 18: 18-19; Jeremiah 37: 6-10.

[20] Mengestu, *God as Father in Paul*, 138-139.

of one another, by calling God the Father of not just the Jewish people but also of all people, "the Father of all."[21]

Chapter 2 Discussion Questions

1. Compare the Old Testament Revelation of God as creator and ultimate ruler with the how the Greeks and Romans understood creation and leadership among the gods. Include the following in your response: creation, competition, violence, filicide, patricide, *creatio ex nihilo*, *creatio ex materia*, and *creatio continua*, and creation as a home.

2. Compare the Israelite understanding of the Sinai covenant with how a contract is typically defined. Include the following in your response: equal parties, unequal parties, breaking moral laws in the context of a marital relationship, and why the Israelites were chosen.

3. Compare how Davidic kings were understood by the Jewish people as sons of God with how the ancient Greeks, Romans, Egyptians and Asiatic people

---

[21] Mengestu, *God as Father in Paul*, 156. "This can be seen from the way Philo refers to God: "the primal God and Father of all" (Abr 74–75), "the Father of the Universe" (Abr 121), "the Father of all" (Abr 204; Spec. 1.14; Spec 3.127), "Father and Maker of all" (Abr 9, 58), "Maker and Father and Ruler" (Spec 1. 34), "Maker and Father of all," (Spec 2.6), and "the supreme Father of gods and men and the Maker of the whole universe" (Spec 2.165)."

perceived their kings as sons of God. Include the following in your response: absolute rulers, moral law, fraternal manner of perceiving kings, God as father of individuals other than kings.

Chapter 3

God the Father in the New Testament

Introduction

The frequency of the times God is called Father in the New Testament indicates the importance in the New Testament of understanding God as Father. God is called Father 42 times in Matthew, 4 times in Mark, 22 times in Luke, 140 times in Johannine writings (when including John, the letters of John and Revelation), 45 times in the letters of St. Paul (when the letter to the Hebrews is included), and 7 times in the other epistles.[1]

In these instances where the New Testament refers to God as Father, the accent is on God as Jesus's father in a singular sense and God as Father in a plural sense with respect to everyone else. This is particularly evident when Jesus teaches his disciples to pray to "Our Father in heaven" and not to "My Father in heaven."

We will now begin to examine how belief in God as Father shaped the followers of Jesus' relation-ships with one another. In so doing, we will see that Jesus willed a visible community that is united by one common, heavenly Father. The people of this visible community with the common Heavenly Father are to exhibit distinctive qualities which set them apart from all other societies and

---

[1] Abera M. Mengestu, *God as Father in Paul* (Eugene: Pickwick Publications, 2013), 17.

groupings of people. Finally, we will briefly reflect on why Jesus willed His Church to be directed to and united by His Heavenly Father.

Visible Christian Community United by the Heavenly Father

Fr. Eusebe Menard, O.F.M., in commenting on the Our Father points out that, "It is noteworthy that the prayer that Jesus taught his followers is a collective, not an individual, prayer. We do not pray 'My Father…give me this day my daily bread.' Jesus taught us to say, 'Our Father…give us this day our daily bread…forgive us our trespasses, as we forgive…lead us not into temptation, but deliver us from evil.' To be a son and daughter of the Father is to be a brother or sister with Jesus, and with each other."[2] Acknowledging God as our common father transforms how we view those around us. Because God is our Father, I, in Christ, am an adopted son of God. In addition, my neighbors, who are equally sons and daughters of God, are my brothers and sisters.[3]

That our neighbors are our brothers and sisters means that our relationship to God necessarily occurs within the context of a community which we call the Church. The Church, affirms Catholicism, is not only a spiritual community of believers in which God relates primarily to the individual in a uniquely internal manner, as various forms of Protestantism have held, but also is a "visible society"

---

[2] Eusebe Menard, *Spiritual Directory*, 41.

[3] 1 John 3:1 "See what love the Father has given us, that we should be called children of God…." (NRSV)

along with being a "spiritual community."[4] As the Vatican II's *Sacrosanctum Concilium* defines, "It is of the essence of the Church that she be both human and divine, visible and yet invisibly equipped, eager to act and yet intent on contemplation, present in this world and yet not at home in it."[5]

Gerhard Lohfink brings to our attention that when Jesus refers to this new community of brothers and sisters with God as our common Father, He promises we will gain numerous brothers, sisters, mothers and children while omitting fathers from His list of relations. In Mark, Jesus promises, "'Truly I tell you,' ... 'no one who has left home or brothers or sisters or mother or father or children or fields for me and the gospel will fail to receive a hundred times as much in this present age: homes, brothers, sisters, mothers, children and fields—along with persecutions—and in the age to come eternal life.'"[6] (Mark 10:29-30 NRSV) This omission, interprets Lohfink, reflects Je-

---

[4] "*Catechism of the Catholic Church*," no. 771, vatican.va, http://www.vatican.va/archive/ccc_css/archive/catechism/p123a9p1.htm; Gerhard Lohfink, *Jesus and Community: The Social Dimension of Christian Faith*, trans. John P. Galvin (Philadelphia: Fortress Press, 1984), loc. 72.

[5] "Constitution on the Sacred Liturgy: *Sacrosanctum Concilium*, December 4, 1963," no. 2, vatican.va, http://www.vatican.va/archive/hist_councils/ii_vatican_council/documents/vat-ii_const_19631204_sacrosanctum-concilium_en.html.

[6] Gerhard Lohfink, *Jesus and Community: The Social Dimension of Christian Faith*, trans. John P. Galvin (Philadelphia: Fortress Press, 1984), loc. 558.

sus' request in Matthew:

> not to be called rabbi, for you have one teacher, and you are all students. And call no one your father on earth, for you have one Father—the one in heaven. Nor are you to be called instructors, for you have one instructor, the Messiah. The greatest among you will be your servant. All who exalt themselves will be humbled, and all who humble themselves will be exalted. (Matthew 23:8-12 NRSV)

The use of hyperbole by the Jewish people needs to be remembered when interpreting the above words of Jesus. Several chapters earlier, Jesus, quoting from the prophet Hosea says, "I desire mercy, not sacrifice." (Matthew 9:13 NRSV) In accordance with the common use of hyperbole, Hosea and Jesus do not mean that sacrifices are to cease. As Amy-Jill Levine explains, they are not saying "I want this [mercy] instead of that [sacrifice]." Rather, they are saying "This [mercy] is more important than that [sacrifice]."[7] Both are to be practiced while prioritizing mercy over sacrifice. Similarly, Jesus, in accordance with hyperbolic speech, is not teaching in Matthew 23 that the title father, rabbi or instructor are not to be used.

Rather, he is teaching that only God is a father and teacher in the fullest sense. All others are only fathers and teachers in a secondary, participatory manner, and, consequently, in their relations with one another are brothers and sisters to each other more than they are fathers and

---

[7] Amy-Jill Levine, The Old Testament, Transcript Book (Chantilly: The Teaching Company, 2001), 310.

teachers to one another. These fraternal bonds which are open to all people regardless of ethnicity are evident right in whom Jesus chose to be his Twelve Apostles. The universal symbolism of the Twelve Apostles is represented in their coming from various regions of Israel and in their diverse backgrounds that were in tension with one another, as is particularly the case with Simon the Zealot and Matthew the tax collector.[8]

---

[8] "Some evidence suggests that Jesus deliberately chose the Twelve from different regions of the country and from different factions within the Judaism of the day in order to make obvious the gathering of all Israelites. The Twelve must have been an odd mixture-from Matthew the tax collector (Matt. 10:3) to Simon the Zealot (Luke 6:15). Including both a tax collector and a Zealot in a single group united the most opposed forces that existed anywhere in Israel at the time, for the tax collectors collaborated with the Romans, while the Zealots emphatically rejected the Roman occupation as incompatible with the reign of God." Gerhard Lohfink, *Jesus and Community: The Social Dimension of Christian Faith*, trans. John P. Galvin (Philadelphia: Fortress Press, 1984), loc. 159. The first reading from Isaiah chapter eight refers to "the land of Zebulun and the land of Naphtali." These lands are important because they are lands of two tribes of Israel: Zebulun and Naphtali.[8] These two tribes are named after two of the sons of Jacob, (renamed Israel). Jacob had 12 sons. The 12 tribes, including the two we just mentioned, stem from Jacob's 12 sons.

Brant Pitre provides biblical evidence that Jesus deliberately chose the Twelve in a certain order and from spe-

The choosing of the Twelve Apostles also signifies

---

cific lands to indicate that He was fulfilling the Old Testament prophecy of a Messiah who would gather back all the tribes of Israel back into one people. For this reason, explains Pitre, Jesus "withdrew to Galilee" after he "heard that John [the Baptist] had been arrested." (Matthew 4:12 NAB) Matthew's gospel then explains that Jesus withdrew to Galilee to fulfill Isaiah prophecy that the Messiah would come from the lands of Zebulun and Naphtali which are both located in Roman Province of Galilee in northern Israel. The other two provinces were, Judea in the South, and Samaria in the north.

According to Isaiah's prophecy (Isaiah 8 and 9), beginning with the tribe of Zebulun and Naphtali, the two tribes that were first defeated and deported by the Assyrians in 722 BC, God will restore his people. Jesus begins to fulfill this prophecy by going to the lands of these two tribes. There, walking by the Sea of Galilee, he called the first two apostles of the 12 Apostles. With this action Jesus signified that he is coming to gather all the 12 tribes together into one people. He is going to restore all of Israel, including the Ten Tribes, known as the lost tribes of Israel, that were conquered by the Assyrians, deported and scattered. Jesus does this by calling all people from every nation to be part of a New Israel, a New People of God, whose promised land is not to be found here but in the life to come. Brant Pitre, "3rd Sunday in Ordinary Time (Year A)," https://store.catholicproductions.com/collections/mass-readings-explained-videos/products/jesus-public-life-begins-galilee-and-the-twelve-apostles?mc_cid=a1ad373856&mc_eid=1bbde22f16.

Ch 3: God the Father in the New Testament

that the universal nature of being a disciple of Jesus entails a community dimension since the Old Testament's Twelve Tribes are being transformed by Jesus into a New Israel that in time will be open to all as a universal Church, in other words, the Catholic Church. As the *Catechism of the Catholic Church* states, "The Lord Jesus endowed his community with a structure that will remain until the Kingdom is fully achieved. Before all else there is the choice of the Twelve with Peter as their head. Representing the twelve tribes of Israel, they are the foundation stones of the new Jerusalem."[9] Within the Catholic Church, within the New Israel, within the renewed people of God gathered around Jesus as the living Torah, God is witnessed to not simply individually but also communally as a body of believers united by Jesus.[10] To reduce the here and not yet presence

---

[9] "Catechism of the Catholic Church," no. 765, ccc.usccb.org, http://ccc.usccb.org/flipbooks/catechism/files/assets/basic-html/toc.html. The following scriptural passages are cited: Mt. 19:28; Lk 22:30; Rev. 21:12-14.

[10] "The texts of the New Testament must not be read through the lens of a theological individualism able to imagine the reign of God only as a universal, interior reality in the souls of individual believers scattered over the face of the earth. Foundational to an important strand in the tradition of Old Testament theology is the idea that God has selected a single people out of all the nations of the world in order to make this people a sign of salvation. His interest in the other nations is no way impeded by this. When the people of God shines as a sign among the nations (cf. Isa. 2:1-4), the other nations will learn from God's people; they will come together in Israel in order to

of the Kingdom of God that the Holy Spirit in the Church brings about to a mere, as Lohfink phrases it, "interior

---

participate, in Israel and mediated through Israel, in God's glory. But all this can happen only when Israel really becomes recognizable as a sign of salvation, when God's salvation transforms his people recognizably, tangibly, even visibly. Jesus did not envision the people of God which he sought to gather as a purely spiritual, purely religious community-as a society in human hearts (*societas in cordibus*). Theses of this sort, which are frequently defended either covertly or openly, fail to do justice to his intentions. The discipleship to which Jesus called was not invisible discipleship; his eating with sinners was not invisible eating; his cures of the sick were not invisible cures- no more than his bloody death on the cross was an invisible event. Jesus' effort to gather Israel was very concrete and visible. That Jesus gave the movement no firmly established, institutionally fixed form has nothing to do with "invisible community;" it stems simply from the fact that he was concerned with Israel, which had long since existed as a community before God (though as a sick and fractured community). It is time to summarize. God selected out of the many peoples of the world a single people, precisely in order to make this people a visible sign of salvation. According to biblical theology, God establishes his eschatological rule, which should in principle encompass the entire world, precisely by beginning very small: with a family (in biblical terms: with Abraham), a clan, a group, a small people." Gerhard Lohfink, *Jesus and Community: The Social Dimension of Christian Faith*, trans. John P. Galvin (Philadelphia: Fortress Press, 1984), 365.

reality of in the souls of individual believers scattered over the face of the earth," completely misses the visible, sacramental nature of the Church as a whole.[11]

Distinctive Qualities of the Christian Father Centered Community

Those who follow Christ as a Church with God as the Father are to live in a way that sets them apart from any other community. This is because, Lohfink explains, Catholics "have received God as their father in a new and radical sense."[12] In their new family within the Church, they have one common Father, and many "brothers and sisters, mothers and children."[13] With God as their one Father, the qualities that they are to emphasize when relating to one another are fraternity, motherliness and "childlikeness before God the Father."[14]

---

[11] "Since the Church is in Christ like a sacrament or as a sign and instrument both of a very closely knit union with God and of the unity of the whole human race, it desires now to unfold more fully to the faithful of the Church and to the whole world its own inner nature and universal mission." "*Lumen Gentium*," http://vatican.va/archive/hist_councils/ii_vatican_council/documents/vat-ii_const_19641121_lumen-gentium_en.html.

[12] Gerhard Lohfink, *Jesus and Community: The Social Dimension of Christian Faith*, trans. John P. Galvin (Philadelphia: Fortress Press, 1984), loc. 616.

[13] Ibid.

[14] Ibid.

To the extent members in the Church live out community life in the distinct way that belief in one common heavenly Father entails, they will become, in varying degrees, a sign of contradiction in the world (Luke 2:34). The Church as a sign of contradiction especially challenges what Benedict XVI calls an "age of activism" in which "doing, achieving results, actively planning and producing the world oneself" in an excessively competitive manner is stressed.[15] In the "new social order" of the New Israel, of the Catholic Church, being and doing are to be balanced, harmonized and integrated with one another while remembering that only God is pure act from whom we receive existence by participating in his existence, who is being itself. To the extent we live out our calling as disciples of Christ, knit together corporately as a Body of Christ (1 Corinthians 12), we become what Lohfink calls a "contrast society" of a "new social order."[16]

In contrasting the Church as an alternative, heavenly inspired social order, Lohfink explains that it is not founded upon "the violent structures of the powers of this world which are to rule within it, but rather [upon] reconciliation and brotherhood."[17] The essentially non-violent social order of the Church centered on Jesus entails loving even one's enemies by willing the good of eternal life for all, provocative non-violence, meekness, truth telling, and absence of lust.

---

[15] Joseph Ratzinger, Hans Urs von Balthasar, trans. A. Walker *Mary: the Church at the Source* (San Francisco: Ignatius Press, 2005), 16.

[16] Lohfink, *Jesus and Community*, 543, 622, 702.

[17] Lohfink, *Jesus and Community*, 702.

Ch 3: God the Father in the New Testament

With respect to the first mentioned quality, Bishop Barron, likely influenced by Walter Wink, explains that non-violence is essential to God's nature and is reflected in creating out of nothing, as explained in a previous chapter. Barron applies this divine non-violence principle to Jesus' reaction to violence. Jesus, according to Barron, responds to violence with "provocative non-violence." For example, after Jesus is struck on the face while standing before Annas he responds with, "If I said anything wrong produce the evidence, but if I spoke the truth why hit me?" (John 18: 23 NAB). This provocative non-violent approach to violence is also evident, but in a different complementary manner, in His advice, "You have heard the commandment, 'An eye for an eye, a tooth for a tooth.' But what I say to you is: offer no resistance to injury. When a person strikes you on the right check, turn and offer him the other.'" (Matthew 5: 38-39 NAB)[18] In both cases, Jesus does

---

[18] According to the biblical scholar Walter Wink the Jewish hearers of Jesus's words understood Jesus reference to the "right cheek" as meaning that "Whenever someone strikes you with his right back hand on your right check, then turn your left one to him as well and do not cower in submission. Stand your ground." According to Jewish law, Jews were forbidden to use the left hand except for unclean acts. Even saying hello to someone with the left hand was punishable with a ten-day penance. The only way, therefore, to strike another's right cheek was with the back of the right hand. The point of striking one with a back hand was to insult and humiliate another not to injure them. A backhand blow by the right hand was to remind the one struck to remember their status, to remember their

not react to violence with violence but rather in a non-violent manner that interiorly pricks the aggressor's conscience. This wake-up call to the conscience causes the doer of violence to face his unjust, unreasonable use of violence. In other words, Jesus is not merely being non-violent but rather is non-violent in a particular way, provocatively, which in Latin (*provocare*) means to call forth or to challenge.

Just because Jesus chose not to respond to violence with violence, however, does not necessarily mean all his disciples at all times are to forgo violence. His close disciples, though, are held to this standard more than others in

---

lower role in life. In other words, this strike was to put that person in his place. Ordinarily this humiliating backhand slap was only done to those lower than the striker. The expecting response was to cower in fear and submission to one higher in station to them: slave and master, wife and husband, child and parent, Jew and Roman. Yet here Jesus is counseling his hearers to neither respond with violence by striking back, this could even cause one to lose their life, nor to respond by cowering submissively. Instead, He teaches do not bow your head, instead turn your cheek and stand your ground. Such a response, according to Wink, would cause the abusive individual to take a step back in bewilderment, the striker cannot backhand the other with his right hand again for the one he struck has turned his left check. If he hits the individual with his fist than the strike loses its humiliating feature since by doing so, "he makes the other his equal, acknowledging him as a peer." Walter Wink, *Beyond Just War and Pacifism: Jesus' Nonviolent Way*, Cres.org http://www.cres.org/star/_wink.htm.

a similar way as some people are called to celibacy but not all. To understand Barron's application of provocative non-violence to Jesus' life it is important, therefore, not to universalize this non-violent principle.[19]

With respect to Jesus' characteristic of meekness, that the Church as the Mystical Body of Christ is also to embody, Lohfink writes, "Jesus is gentle and humble of heart. Unlike the rulers of the nations, he does not seek to dominate and overpower his followers (cf. Mark 10:42). He is the servant of all. He lives not for himself, for his power and his interests, but completely and exclusively for God's sake, for God's kingdom."[20] The Scripture passage Lohfink refers to merits quoting. In Mark, "Jesus called them together and said to them: 'You know how among the Gentiles those who seem to exercise authority lord it over them; their great ones make their importance felt. It cannot be like that with you. Anyone among you who aspires to greatness must serve the rest; whoever wants to rank first among you must serve the needs of all. The Son of Man has not come to be served but to serve-to give his life in ransom for the many.'" (Mark 10: 42-45 NAB) For this reason and others, popes, beginning with Gregory the Great, have called themselves *Servus Servorum Dei*, Servant of the Servants of God.

The third characteristic of Jesus that is to be lived out by His Church is being, identifies Lohfink, "absolutely truthful."[21] The reason for this is that Jesus is "the way,

---

[19] Robert Barron, "Bishop Barron on Daniel Berrigan and Non-violence," https://youtu.be/Y-0z2m_NtS8.

[20] Lohfink, *Jesus and Community*, 777.

[21] Lohfink, *Jesus and Community*, 741.

and the truth and the life" (John 14:5 NAB) since he is the truth spoken eternally by the Father in the love of the Holy Spirit. Martyrdom is the ultimate way to bear witness to the truth since the Greek origin of this word literally means witness.

Finally, Jesus, with his perfect human nature united to his divine nature in His divine person, is absent of all lust. For this reason, He commands the members of His Mystical Body the Church to not even look at another with lust. He says, "anyone who looks lustfully at a woman has already committed adultery with her in his thoughts." (Matthew 5: 28 NAB) Jesus' forbidding of lust is related to his provocative non-violence since lust causes one to look at another as an object to be used in at least a manipulatively violent way to satisfy his desires. In contrast, as John Paul II emphasized, we are to love a person as an end in himself because every person is created in the image and likeness of God.

Even though the Church is animated by the Holy Spirit who was sent into her midst at Pentecost, it is not possible for her members to match Jesus' perfect chastity, provocative non-violence, meekness, and truth telling. Our head Jesus, Lohfink reminds us, flawlessly lived this way.[22] In addition, because of Jesus, the immediate community that surrounded Him before His public ministry also lived this in a perfect manner since Mary was Immaculate conceived, and, according to tradition, Joseph was confirmed in grace after his conception.[23] Bearing this fallen reality in

---

[22] Lohfink, *Jesus and Community*, 741.

[23] Reginald Garrigou-Lagrange states, "God Himself and by God alone to fulfil a mission unique in the world.

mind, what Ratzinger calls, echoing St. Augustine in the *City of God*, "a painful 'between' in which the Church in the meantime still stands in,"[24] the Church does not serve as a political model for this world but rather as an icon, as a window into heaven, as a foretaste of a reality to comes, she shines forth like "a city set on a hill,"[25] a different social order whose fullness does not belong to this world but to the Heavenly Jerusalem. The Church represents the heavenly Jerusalem, the Kingdom of God in a here and not yet perfected state.

Reasons for the Christian Father Centered Community

The reason for the Church's presence in the world is precisely because of the world to come at the end of time when at Christ's Second Coming the heavenly dimension will be fully wedded to earthly realities thereby transforming the earthly dimension into a "New Earth". (Revelation 21: 1 NAB) In her present here and not yet state, the

---

We cannot say at what precise moment St. Joseph's sanctification took place. But we can say that, from the time of his marriage to Our Lady, he was confirmed in grace, because of his special mission." Reginald Garrigou-Lagrange, *The Mother of the Saviour*, trans. Bernard J. Kelly (St. Louis: B. Herder Book Company, 1949), chapter 7.

[24] Joseph Ratzinger, *Das Neue Volk Gottes* (Düsseldorf: Patmos-Verlag, 1969), 167. " ...das bedeutet das schmerzliche „Zwischen", in dem die Kirche einstweilen noch steht."

[25] Matthew 5:14 NAB

Church participates in the mission of Christ who gave glory on earth to His Heavenly Father by completing the work the Father gave him. (John 17: 4)

The Church fulfills her mission as a community which glorifies the Heavenly Father by being other centered. As the New Israel, she was not chosen for her own sake but chosen for the sake of all people, so that all people, including Israel, which was chosen before the gentiles, would one day belong to the Catholic Church of Jesus Christ. In this sense, explains Lohfink the Catholic Church is not "a substitute or replacement for Israel." Instead, the Church is intended by Christ "to remain open to Israel and constantly directed toward the whole of Israel" for the time foretold by St. Paul when Israel "will be saved." (Romans 11:26 NAB)[26]

---

[26] Lohfink, *Jesus and Community*, 994. "It was to prefigure eschatological Israel, to represent symbolically what really should have taken place in Israel as a whole. In view of Jesus' stubborn claim on the whole of Israel, any ecclesiology which fails to work out the permanent relationship of church and synagogue in salvation history must be called into question as unfaithful to Jesus. ... 1. It was precisely through Israel's failure that salvation came to the nations (11:11). It was precisely through Israel's failure that the Gentiles were brought into Israel's history of election (11:13-24). 2. Israel's failure is depicted to the church as a permanent warning."

Chapter 3 Discussion Questions

1. Interpret Matthew 23:8-12 in a Catholic manner. Include the following in your response: hyperbole, Matthew 9:13, God as Father, fatherhood among men, brotherhood among men.

2. Discuss the distinctive qualities of Catholic communities. Include the following in your response: sign of contradiction, new social order, worldly political order, violence, truth, love, and chastity.

3. In reference to Romans 11:26, discuss the relationship of Israel to the Church. Include the following in your answer: Israel, Gentiles, New Israel, and chosen for the sake of others.

Chapter 4

Post-Apostolic and Post-Constantine Church

Introduction

In this chapter, we will study how in time the Church grounded by Jesus in the Fatherhood of God as a Catholic Church retained its essential identity. We will do so in two parts. First, we will study the Catholic Church in the Post-Apostolic times[1] through the writings of selected early Church Fathers and Christian writers that Gerhard Lohfink refers to in *Jesus and Community*. Then, we will focus our attention on the Church in the Post-Constantine times, which includes our present age.

Early Church of the Church Fathers and Early Christian Writers

In the following excerpts of Saint Justin Martyr (100-165), qualities that set Christians as a community apart from other people are identified. They include sharing with the needy, living chastely, loving and praying for enemies, avoiding war and violence, speaking truthfully, and witnessing to Christ even to the point of martyrdom:

---

[1] According to tradition, John the Apostle in 100 AD was the last Apostle to die.

And the wealthy among us help the needy; and we always keep together; and for all things wherewith we are supplied, we bless the Maker of all through His Son Jesus Christ, and through the Holy Ghost.[2]

...[W]e also, since our persuasion by the Word, stand aloof from them (i.e., the demons), and follow the only unbegotten God through His Son--we who formerly delighted in fornication, but now embrace chastity alone; we who formerly used magical arts, dedicate ourselves to the good and unbegotten God; we who valued above all things the acquisition of wealth and possessions, now bring what we have into a common stock, and communicate to everyone in need; we who hated and destroyed one another, and on account of their different manners would not live with men of a different tribe, now, since the coming of Christ, live familiarly with them, and pray for our enemies, and endeavor to persuade those who hate us unjustly to live conformably to the good precepts of Christ, to the end that they may become partakers with us of the same joyful hope of a reward from God the ruler of all...[3]

And when the Spirit of prophecy speaks as predicting things that are to come to pass, He speaks in this way:[4]

---

[2] St. Justin Martyr, "First Apology," chap. LXVII, http://www.earlychristianwritings.com/text/justinmartyr-firstapology.html.

[3] St. Justin Martyr, "First Apology," chap. XIV.

[4] See Isaiah 2.

"For out of Zion shall go forth the law, and the word of the Lord from Jerusalem. And He shall judge among the nations, and shall rebuke many people; and they shall beat their swords into ploughshares, and their spears into pruning-hooks: nation shall not lift up sword against nation, neither shall they learn war anymore." And that it did so come to pass, we can convince you. For from Jerusalem there went out into the world, men, twelve in number, and these illiterate, of no ability in speaking: but by the power of God they proclaimed to every race of men that they were sent by Christ to teach to all the word of God; and we who formerly used to murder one another do not only now refrain from making war upon our enemies, but also, that we may not lie nor deceive our examiners, willingly die confessing Christ. For that saying, "The tongue has sworn but the mind is unsworn," might be imitated by us in this matter. But if the soldiers enrolled by you, and who have taken the military oath, prefer their allegiance to their own life, and parents, and country, and all kindred, though you can offer them nothing incorruptible, it were verily ridiculous if we, who earnestly long for incorruption, should not endure all things, in order to obtain what we desire from Him who is able to grant it.[5]

...[W]e who were filled with war, and mutual slaughter, and every wickedness, have each through the whole earth changed our warlike weapons,--our swords into plough-shares, and our spears into imple-

---

[5] St. Justin Martyr, "First Apology," chap. XXXIX.

ments of tillage,--and we cultivate piety, righteousness, philanthropy, faith, and hope, which we have from the Father Himself through Him who was crucified; and sitting each under his vine, i.e., each man possessing his own married wife. For you are aware that the prophetic word says, 'And his wife shall be like a fruitful vine.' Now it is evident that no one can terrify or subdue us who have believed in Jesus over all the world. For it is plain that, though beheaded, and crucified, and thrown to wild beasts, and chains, and fire, and all other kinds of torture, we do not give up our confession; but the more such things happen, the more do others and in larger numbers become faithful, and worshippers of God through the name of Jesus. For Just as if one should cut away the fruit-bearing parts of a vine, it grows up again, and yields other branches flourishing and fruitful; even so the same thing happens with us.[6]

Saint Aristides (100s) was an early Christian Greek author, who is particularly known for the *Apology of Aristides*. In the following excerpt, he also identifies key distinguishing features of Christians. These include chastity, honesty, honoring one's parents, not coveting, not worshiping idols, treating fellow Christians as brothers and sisters, loving strangers, fasting from food in order to give the food that was fasted from to the poor:

---

[6] Justin Martyr, "Dialogue with Trypho," chap. CX, http://www.earlychristianwritings.com/text/justinmartyr-dialoguetrypho.html.

Ch 4: Post-Apostolic and Post-Constantine Church

But the Christians, ... do not commit adultery nor fornication, nor bear false witness, nor embezzle what is held in pledge, nor covet what is not theirs. They honor father and mother, and show kindness to those near to them; and whenever they are judges, they judge uprightly. They do not worship idols (made) in the image of man; and whatsoever they would not that others should do unto them, they do not to others; and of the food which is consecrated to idols they do not eat, for they are pure. And their oppressors they appease (lit: comfort) and make them their friends; they do good to their enemies; and their women, O King, are pure as virgins, and their daughters are modest; and their men keep themselves from every unlawful union and from all uncleanness, in the hope of a recompense to come in the other world. Further, if one or other of them have bondmen and bondwomen or children, through love towards them they persuade them to become Christians, and when they have done so, they call them brethren without distinction. They do not worship strange gods, and they go their way in all modesty and cheerfulness. Falsehood is not found among them; and they love one another, and from widows they do not turn away their esteem; and they deliver the orphan from him who treats him harshly. And he, who has, gives to him who has not, without boasting. And when they see a stranger, they take him in to their homes and rejoice over him as a very brother; for they do not call them brethren after the flesh, but brethren after the spirit and in God. And whenever one of their poor passes from the world, each one of them according to his ability gives heed to him and carefully sees to his burial. And if they hear that one of their number is imprisoned or afflicted on account of the name of their Messiah, all of them anxiously minister to his necessity, and if it is possible to redeem him they set him free. And if there is among them any that is poor and needy, and if they have no spare food, they fast two or three days in order to supply to the needy their lack of food. … And further if they see that any one of them dies in his ungodliness or in his sins, for him they grieve bitterly, and sorrow as for one who goes to meet his doom.[7]

Athenagoras (c. 133-190) was a Greek Christian who is recognized by the Orthodox as a saint. The distinct Christian characteristics he describes include the following: adherence to truth, love of enemies, even by blessing and praying for them, and avoiding civil law courts. The early Christian practice of avoiding civil courts is important to keep in mind in our highly litigious age:

If I go minutely into the particulars of our doctrine, let it not surprise you. It is that you may not be carried away by the popular and irrational opinion, but may have the truth clearly before you. For presenting the opinions themselves to which we adhere, as being not human but uttered and taught by God, we shall be able to persuade you not to think of us as atheists. What, then, are those teachings in which we are

---

[7] Aristides, "The Apology of Aristides the Philosopher," XV, http://www.earlychristianwritings.com/text/aristides-kay.html.

brought up? I say unto you, Love your enemies; bless them that curse you; pray for them that persecute you; that you may be the sons of your Father who is in heaven, who causes His sun to rise on the evil and the good, and sends rain on the just and the unjust. Luke 6:27-28; Matthew 5:44-45 Allow me here to lift up my voice boldly in loud and audible outcry, pleading as I do before philosophic princes. For who of those that reduce syllogisms, and clear up ambiguities, and explain etymologies, or of those who teach homonyms and synonyms, and predicaments and axioms, and what is the subject and what the predicate, and who promise their disciples by these and such like instructions to make them happy: who of them have so purged their souls as, instead of hating their enemies, to love them; and, instead of speaking ill of those who have reviled them (to abstain from which is of itself an evidence of no mean forbearance), to bless them; and to pray for those who plot against their lives? On the contrary, they never cease with evil intent to search out skillfully the secrets of their art, and are ever bent on working some ill, making the art of words and not the exhibition of deeds their business and profession. But among us you will find uneducated persons, and artisans, and old women, who, if they are unable in words to prove the benefit of our doctrine, yet by their deeds exhibit the benefit arising from their persuasion of its truth: they do not rehearse speeches, but exhibit good works; when struck, they do not strike again; when robbed, they do not go to law; they give to those that ask of them, and love their neighbors as themselves.[8]

In his *Apology*, the early Christian writer Tertullian (c. 155-240) identifies what makes the Christian community distinct and separate from all other communities. He begins by describing the Christian community as one body that is united by one faith, a "common hope," and one love that unites the body together in an orderly, disciplined manner. More specific features include praying for those who persecute Christians, including the emperors, not buying ecclesiastical offices, voluntarily contributing to Church funds, aiding the poor with the funds collected, viewing fellow Christians as brothers, and sharing goods in common except wives.

> I shall at once go on, then, to exhibit the peculiarities of the Christian society, that, as I have refuted the evil charged against it, I may point out its positive good. We are a body knit together as such by a common religious profession, by unity of discipline, and by the bond of a common hope. We meet together as an assembly and congregation, that, offering up prayer to God as with united force, we may wrestle with Him in our supplications. This violence God delights in. We pray, too, for the emperors, for their ministers and for all in authority, for the welfare of the world, for the prevalence of peace, for the delay of the final consummation. ... The tried men of our elders preside

---

[8] Athenagoras, "A Plea for the Christians," chap. 11, http://www.newadvent.org/fathers/0205.htm.

over us, obtaining that honor not by purchase, but by established character. There is no buying and selling of any sort in the things of God. Though we have our treasure-chest, it is not made up of purchase-money, as of a religion that has its price. On the monthly day, if he likes, each puts in a small donation; but only if it be his pleasure, and only if he be able: for there is no compulsion; all is voluntary. These gifts are, as it were, piety's deposit fund. For they are not taken thence and spent on feasts, and drinking-bouts, and eating-houses, but to support and bury poor people, to supply the wants of boys and girls destitute of means and parents, and of old persons confined now to the house; such, too, as have suffered shipwreck; and if there happen to be any in the mines, or banished to the islands, or shut up in the prisons, for nothing but their fidelity to the cause of God's Church, they become the nurslings of their confession. But it is mainly the deeds of a love so noble that lead many to put a brand upon us. See, they say, how they love one another, for themselves are animated by mutual hatred; how they are ready even to die for one another, for they themselves will sooner put to death. And they are angry with us, too, because we call each other brethren; for no other reason, as I think, than because among themselves names of consanguinity are assumed in mere pretence of affection. But we are your brethren as well, by the law of our common mother nature, though you are hardly men, because brothers so unkind. At the same time, how much more fittingly they are called and counted brothers who have been led to the knowledge of God as their common Father, who have drunk in one spirit of holiness, who from the same womb of a common ignorance have agonized into the same light of truth! … One in mind and soul, we do not hesitate to share our earthly goods with one another. All things are common among us but our wives. … … We are in our congregations just what we are when separated from each other; we are as a community what we are individuals; we injure nobody, we trouble nobody.[9]

Origen (c. 184-253) is another early Christian writer who also contrasted Christians with non-Christians. He argues that even the least exemplary of Christians are often more virtuous than many non-Christians.

Whereas the Churches of God which are instructed by Christ, when carefully contrasted with the assemblies of the districts in which they are situated, are as beacons in the world; for who would not admit that even the inferior members of the Church, and those who in comparison with the better are less worthy, are nevertheless more excellent than many of those who belong

---

[9] Tertullian, " Apology," chap. 39, newadvent.org, http://www.newadvent.org/fathers/0301.htm. The source cited is as follows. Translated by S. Thelwall. From Ante-Nicene Fathers, Vol. 3. Edited by Alexander Roberts, James Donaldson, and A. Cleveland Coxe. (Buffalo, NY: Christian Literature Publishing Co., 1885.) Revised and edited for New Advent by Kevin Knight. http://www.newadvent.org/fathers/0301.htm.

to the assemblies in the different districts?[10]

Eusebius (c.260-339) was a Greek Christian writer, who is particularly known as a historian. In his book *Church History,* he contrasts Christians with non-Christians by comparing how the two groups treated those who have contracted a disease. Unlike non-Christians, Christians did not abandon those who were sick but courageously cared for them even if this meant risking getting sick themselves.

> …[H]e [Dionysius] adds 'The most of our brethren were unsparing in their exceeding love and brotherly kindness. They held fast to each other and visited the sick fearlessly, and ministered to them continually, serving them in Christ. And they died with them most joyfully, taking the affliction of others, and drawing the sickness from their neighbors to themselves and willingly receiving their pains. And many who cared for the sick and gave strength to others died themselves having transferred to themselves their death. … But with the heathen everything was quite otherwise. They deserted those who began to be sick, and fled from their dearest friends. And they cast them out into the streets when they were half dead, and left the dead like refuse, unburied. They shunned any participation or fellowship with death; which yet, with all their precautions, it was not easy for them to escape.[11]

---

[10] Origen, "Contra Celsus," book III, chap. 29, http://www.newadvent.org/fathers/ 04163.htm.

[11] Eusebius, "Church History," book VII, chap. 22, http://www.newadvent.org/fathers/ 250107.htm.

You may have noticed that all the Fathers and early Christian writers who were selected above lived before 313. 313 was the year when, with the proclamation of the Edict of Milan, persecution of Christians ended and Christianity became an accepted religion to practice in the Roman Empire. Explanations abound as to why Christians were persecuted prior to the Edict of Milan, including Rene Girard's scapegoating theory and the explanation that many Roman Emperors persecuted Christians out of interest of state security which they believed Christians were undermining. While these and other explanations may be true in varying ways, it is important to bear in mind the biblical reason why the just are persecuted. According to the Book of Wisdom, chapter two, the righteous are persecuted because they deeply disturb the consciences of those who refuse to repent. The disturbed consciences of the unrepentant causes them to react by expelling and even killing saintly people:

> Let us lie in wait for the righteous man, because he is inconvenient to us and opposes our actions; he reproaches us for sins against the law, and accuses us of sins against our training. He professes to have knowledge of God, and calls himself a child of the Lord. He became to us a reproof of our thoughts; the very sight of him is a burden to us, because his manner of life is unlike that of others, and his ways are strange. We are considered by him as something base, and he avoids our ways as unclean; he calls the last end of the righteous happy, and boasts that God is his father. Let us see if his words are true, and let us test

what will happen at the end of his life; for if the righteous man is God's child, he will help him, and will deliver him from the hand of his adversaries. Let us test him with insult and torture, so that we may find out how gentle he is, and make trial of his forbearance. Let us condemn him to a shameful death, for, according to what he says, he will be protected. (Wisdom 2: 12-20 NRSV)

In accordance with this Biblical explanation Lohfink writes, "Those who have been sanctified by Christ and live in his truth are therefore sharply distinguished from the rest of society, from its deceit, its institutionalized untruth. They will be hated by others since they expose the social construction of reality as deceit."[12] Heeding Romans 12:2, therefore, Christians are not to be "conformed to this world." (NRSV) Lohfink translates this passage as, "Do not make yourselves like the structures (literally, the form) of this age."[13] The more a Christian community assimilates without discernment by aping and mimicking the structures, and forms of non-Christian organizations, such as from the corporate world, from the military, or from state government, the less of a prophetic witness Catholicism will be of the Kingdom of God that is here but in a to be perfected state.[14]

---

[12] Gerhard Lohfink, *Jesus and Community: The Social Dimension of Christian Faith*, trans. John P. Galvin (Philadelphia: Fortress Press, 1984), loc. 1634.

[13] Lohfink, *Jesus and Community*, loc. 1595.

[14] Abbot Vonier provides a related explanation for why persecution occurs. Sometimes, the Holy Spirit sends

The inverse can also occur where the state tries to imitate the here and not yet reality of the Church by attempting to be a perfect society in the here and now without reference to a heavenly dimension that transcends this world. An early example of this occurred under Emperor Julian, nicknamed Julian the Apostate (361-363). As emperor, he revived persecution of Christians by reopening pagan temples, and, in competition with Christianity, by establishing charitable works run by the state including hostels, and assistance programs for the poor.[15] Although Julian overturned the pro-Christian Roman state policy

---

the Church as the Mystical Body of Christ into a desert, representing times of persecution, to purify Her. He writes, "It is indeed a positive relief to one's mind to be able to have this faith in the divinely appointed mission of temptation. It sets one free from the incubus of a false historical presentment of the long life of the Catholic Church. The countless difficulties that have beset her course are not of necessity the result of her shortcomings; a most perfect Church may be carried hither and thither by evil agencies, as the spotless body of Christ was taken through the air, His soul, of course, remaining untouched by the hands of the tempter. No true reading of Christianity is possible except in the light of the theology of temptation. But once that light is thrown on the apparently checkered career of Catholicism, as a beam from a lighthouse, what a difference of meaning and outline appears!" Abbot Vonier, *Christianus: The Christian Life* (Bethesda: Zaccheus Press, 1933), loc. 1033.

[15] R. Joseph Hoffmann, *Julian's Against the Galileans* (Amherst: Prometheus Books, 2004), 12-17, 31-32.

begun by Constantine, his anti-Christian policy did not last long since his reign lasted only about two years. Providentially, Julian was replaced by a pro-Christian emperor, Jovian, who once again brought an end to Julian's anti-Christian policy. A more modern example is Karl Marx's communism, which Hans Urs von Balthasar called "secularized Jewish messianism."[16]

Post-Constantine Church

During the pre-Constantinian age, when Catholicism was openly persecuted, Catholicism gained adherents not so much through missionary activity but rather by their witness as a loving, faith filled, truth centered community whose hope is in a divine reality that surpasses any earthly kingdom. In the Post-Constantinian Church, with occasional exceptions, missionary activity became a possibility and, consequently, occurred. Both the missionary emphasis during post-Constantinian times, which has more of a

---

[16] Warren H. Carroll, *The Building of Christendom, A History of Christendom, vol. 2* (Front Royal: Christendom College Press, 1987), 53-54; Von Balthasar writes, "Marx's project of a 'positive humanism," which he thinks will result primarily from economic change, is secularized Jewish messianism. It is secularized because it no longer rests on liberation by Yahweh from the house of bondage, but is bent on producing man's absolute freedom by man's own power, with the goal of eliminating all dependence on anyone or anything." Han Urs von Balthasar, "The Absoluteness of Christianity and the Catholicity of the Church," *Communio* 40 (Spring 2013), 156.

pronounced individual aspect than previously, and the community witness of the Post-Constantinian era, are complementary ways to fulfill Jesus' command to "Go into the whole world and proclaim the good news to all creation." (Mark 16:15 NAB) It is not a question of choosing one over the other but rather of affirming both as needed in salvation history.

Sadly, many have forgotten the unique corporate, community witness as a body of Christ, which the early Christians frequently wrote on and were especially aware of. As Abbot Vonier states, "If Christians have been good individually, as a Church they have failed miserably. Such is the modern verdict."[17] This modern verdict is contrary to what Scripture teaches regarding Pentecost, for at Pentecost the Holy Spirit was sent into the midst of the disciples to enliven and unite them in a way no human community ever has or will be united.[18] Because of Pentecost, argues Vonier, "the Church through her daily works [is] to be a demonstration of the Spirit's activities in her." This, he asserts, "is a matter of life and death. If she is not a sign of the Paraclete, she is nothing."[19] The Church is not nothing since God has given her a unique relationship with the Holy Spirit which will last throughout time, for the "gates of hell shall not prevail against it." (Matthew 16:18 DRA)

Because of her relationship with the Holy Spirit, the Church is the Bride of Christ (Revelation 21:2), and, consequently, His mystical body (1 Cor. 12:12-27; Ephesians

---

[17] Dom Anscar Vonier, *The Spirit and the Bride* (Assumption Press, 2013), Loc. 154.

[18] Vonier, *The Spirit and the Bride*, Loc. 185.

[19] Vonier, *The Spirit and the Bride*, Loc. 404.

5:30).[20] Other New Testament metaphors describing the Church include the Church as a New Jerusalem, as a City of God (Revelation 21:2), House of God (1 Tim. 3:15) and as "holy and immaculate, without stain or wrinkle or anything of that sort." (Ephesians 5:27 NAB) Often, these metaphors are misunderstood by interpreting them to signify the Church as she is perfected in heaven. However, as Vonier explains, this is incorrect since Paul intended that these metaphors apply not only to the Church in her perfected state in heaven but also to her pilgrim state on earth. This does not mean that the Church in all her members on earth are without blemish. What it does mean is that the Church as a community of believers is without blemish because of the Holy Spirit, Who enlivens her and unites her on earth. The perfect example of this is Mary, who often is identified with the Church.[21]

The Holy Spirit was given to the Church at Pentecost as, explains Vonier, "an entirely new event and also a final one. No other incident of equal magnitude has ever existed in the realm of the Spirit, nor will there be another supernatural event as great, till Christ comes in glory and majesty, to judge the living and the dead."[22] Due to the gift of the Holy Spirit to the Church at Pentecost, the day of Pentecost is traditionally held to be the Church's birthday, but not in a way that precludes her anticipation in the Old Testament.[23] On her birthday, the Holy Spirit transformed

---

[20] Vonier, *The Spirit and the Bride*, Loc. 560.

[21] Vonier, *The Spirit and the Bride*, Loc. 533, 781.

[22] Vonier, *The Spirit and the Bride*, Loc. 838.

[23] Vonier, *The Spirit and the Bride*, Loc. 801, 883. "We are not disciples who follow the Lord on the dusty road

individual disciples gathered around Mary into a Church that Vonier describes "is a profoundly social godliness."[24]

---

during His public ministry, we are not even disciples who eat and drink with Him during the forty days that follow Easter, but we are the elect of God, who walk with the risen Christ in newness of life, that newness of life which the Apostles themselves did not possess till the Spirit came down upon them at Pentecost. In many ways, of course, we imitate the disciples as they are the companions of the mortal Christ and the risen Christ before the ascension, but such an imitation, however high a spirituality it may be, is far from being a total Christianity. We actually share in Christ's risen life, we share in Christ's ascension; we are not only His friends and admirers in those auspicious periods of His wonderful career:"

[24] Vonier, *The Spirit and the Bride*, Loc. 898. "At Pentecost, then, the Holy Ghost added something essential, something substantial, to all that had been done by Him in the times past. He came and united Himself with that chosen portion of mankind called the Church, in a most manifest fashion: the baptism of the Spirit, as evident a distinction as had been the baptism of John, was bestowed on chosen men. In the days of the Precursor, men went about who gloried in the fact that they had been baptized by John; they were found all over the world. With the coming of the Spirit a new society sprang up, the society of those that were baptized in the Spirit, as the Lord foretold. When we say that the Church was born on the day of Pentecost, we mean of course that the beginning of a life which is a total life, which is the whole new sanctity of Christianity, was started then; not only were external signs

This social godliness and the holiness of individual members is due to the "fundamental constitutional principle of the Church, that special presence of the Holy Ghost which is the Church's unique privilege."[25] A direct consequence of the special presence of the Holy Spirit is the Church being a "sign of Christ's resurrection."[26]

Since the Holy Spirit is the fundamental principle of the Church, when many members of the Church decline in virtue to such an extent that there is a great need for renewal of the Church, the Church is not renewed by, writes Vonier, "an unexpected help from the outside, as if suddenly forces came into the Church that had not been there before."[27] Rather, she is always renewed by looking within

---

given of the presence of the Spirit, but an internal holiness, the holiness of the Church, began its mighty career on that day; it is the birth of Pentecostal holiness, a sanctity which has all the elements of the ancient godliness and much more. What that excess is, it is difficult to describe adequately; but no doubt the essence of the new holiness is this: the oneness of charity of all those that invoke the Name of Christ and constitute the Church. This is what St. Paul calls "drinking the same Spirit" (1 Cor 10: 4). It is a profoundly social godliness, it is the "new commandment," the precept of mutual love which the Spirit with flaming power forces the disciples to obey: "A new commandment I give you, that you love each other as I have loved you" (John 13: 34)."

[25] Vonier, *The Spirit and the Bride*, Loc. 1185.

[26] Vonier, *The Spirit and the Bride*, Loc. 781.

[27] Vonier, *The Spirit and the Bride*, Loc. 1372. Vonier cautions against an excessively critical view of the Church

66 *God as Father & Priests as Fathers, Brothers, Bridegrooms & Disciples*

herself, by relying on the special presence of the Holy Spirit that she was given at Pentecost in a new, abiding, and definitive manner.[28] While in her pilgrim state on earth, which St Augustine defines as a mixed body (*corpus mixtum*) of sin and holiness within her members, the Church is always in need of renewal.[29] Renewal of the Church may

---

since, "To enumerate the sins of the Christian people and not to speak of their repentances is the conduct one generally ascribes to the spirit of darkness, Satan, who is called in the Scriptures "the accuser of the brethren of the elect" (Rev 12:10), accusing them before the throne of God day and night." Vonier, *The Spirit and the Bride*, Loc. 988. He also points out that, "So much of the criticism of the Church's ways by her own sons, is concerned, not with absolute values, but with relative values. ..." Vonier, *The Spirit and the Bride*, Loc. 988.

[28] Vonier, *The Spirit and the Bride*, Loc. 1410. "[T]he coming of the Spirit at the first Pentecost was meant to be an entirely new event and also a final one. No other incident of equal magnitude has ever existed in the realm of the Spirit, nor will there be another supernatural event as great, till Christ comes in glory and majesty, to judge the living and the dead." Vonier, *The Spirit and the Bride*, Loc. 838. "The Holy Ghost, like the Word, came once: He does not come a second time; after His coming He abides, and it is this abiding presence that is the constant renewal of life; not a fresh advent like the one of the first Pentecost." Vonier, *The Spirit and the Bride*, Loc. 1410.

[29] Vonier, *The Spirit and the Bride*, Loc. 2289. St. Augustine description of the pilgrim Church as a *corpus mixtum* was formed during and after his fight against the Donatist

involve reforming the moral lives of its members, in other words rooting out moral worldliness such as was evident in some Popes of both the 9th and 10th century and during the Renaissance.

However, this is not the only reform that the Church undergoes. Another reform, identified by Vonier, is rooting out spiritual worldliness which is much more deceptive since on the outside members appear morally upright, but on the inside their apparent virtue is not true virtue since they are being virtuous for worldly reasons, such as honors they will receive in the Church and outside of the Church for being decent men, or using the Church to build up a nation.[30] Vonier goes so far as to claim, "Even if men were

---

heresy which held that the validity of sacraments depend on the holiness of the priest. Charles Mathewes, *Books That Matter, The City of God* (Chantilly: The Teaching Company, 2016), 79, 391-392. See Book 19, Chapters 17 and 26 of the *City of God*. Augustine distinguishes the two cities by making a distinction, explains Chad Pecknold, "between the social (higher) and the political (lower)" orders. For this reason, Catholic tradition, providentially influenced by this distinction has consistently seen the social or societal order as greater than the political order since the political order is directed to earthly peace while social order ought to be directed to the peace whose fullness is only present in the heavenly Jerusalem. C.C. Pecknold, *Christianity and Politics: A Brief Guide to the History* (Eugene: Cascade Books, 2010), 48, 124.

[30] Vonier, *The Spirit and the Bride*, Loc. 1730. "If it were the business of the Church exclusively to foster a nation's greatness, even if it were of a spiritual order, how could

filled with every spiritual perfection, but if such perfections were not referred to God (suppose this hypothesis to be possible), it would be unredeemed worldliness."[31] Vonier identifies the ultimate of unredeemed spiritual worldliness as apostasy from the faith.[32] A theoretical example is a member in the Church, perhaps even a cleric, who leaves an almost impeccable moral life but does not believe. What motivates this hidden apostate to practice his faith is what can be gained by his status in the Church.

In her pilgrim, *corpus mixtum* state, the Catholic Church is always in need of renewal, renewal that takes place by relying on the special gift of the Holy Spirit given to the Church at Pentecost. Sometimes, those who are intent on reforming the Church can fall into an error that Lohfink warns against, the error of attempting to transform "the church into a religious achievement society."[33] An important distinction that Augustine formulated can help those wanting to renew the Church to avoid misunderstanding the Church as something we improve and create. He made this distinction during and after his struggles with the heretical Donatists who held that the validity of the sacraments depends on the holiness of the priest

Augustine distinguished the social order of the Church that is inspired by the Holy Spirit and directed to the Kingdom of Heaven in a here and not yet state, from the political order of this world that is directed to the earthly

---

the eight beatitudes survive? They are truly incompatible with any greatness except that of the kingdom of heaven."

[31] Vonier, *The Spirit and the Bride*, Loc. 1709.

[32] Vonier, *The Spirit and the Bride*, Loc. 988.

[33] Lohfink, *Jesus and Community*, Loc. 2260.

peace.[34] Since the pilgrim Church is a mixture of holiness and sinfulness, and since the pilgrim Church lives in this world these two orders are mixed within the Church's mixed state on earth. With respect to her social order, the Church, explains Lohfink, is a "creation of the grace of God and fruit of the cross of Christ." This means that:

> [i]n contrast to pagan society [the Church] does not stem from "efficiency and moralism," but from the miracle of the inbreaking reign of God. It is for this reason that the guilty and the unsuccessful have a place in the church, for grace comes to perfection in human impotence. And it is for this reason that the miracle of new creation shines most beautifully in the church when it emerges as love and reconciliation in situations which – seen from a human perspective – seem lost and hopeless.[35]

The holiness of the Church includes both a difference from the world by being set apart as a different social order complete with a different constitutional principle, the Holy Spirit, and the holiness of the Church is Catholic by, in accordance with the Greek word *katholikos* meaning pertaining to the whole, being open to all, especially to "the

---

[34] Vonier, *The Spirit and the Bride*, Loc. 2289; Charles Mathewes, *Books That Matter, The City of God* (Chantilly: The Teaching Company, 2016), 79, 391-392. See Book 19, Chapters 17 and 26 of the *City of God*; C.C. Pecknold, *Christianity and Politics: A Brief Guide to the History* (Eugene: Cascade Books, 2010), 48, 124.

[35] Lohfink, *Jesus and Community*, 2273.

guilty and the unsuccessful." As a Catholic Church, the Church's mission is to be in the world but not of the world as Jesus prayed to His Father, "I do not ask you to take them out of the world, but to guard them from the evil one...As you have sent me into the world, so I have sent them into the world." (John 17:15-18 NAB) Her presence in the world, therefore, is to be like yeast, which does not destroy what it is in but transforms what it is within.

This transformation occurs as the Church identifies all the good that she encounters and then helps to order the goods desired in proper relationship to God, the supreme good, and to our neighbors, made in the image and likeness of God, for, as Augustine taught, sin is loving goods in a disordered way which lead to misery, for example lusting after another man's wife. As a divinely instituted reality, the Church's transformative affect certainly, explains Lohfink, entails being separate as the biblical use of the term implies, but it is "not separated in a ghetto, [like the Qumran community] in religious self-satisfaction or in cultural or intellectual isolation, but separated to a different style of life and to new forms of life which realize what God wants society to be, in contrast to the structures [and people who make up these structures] of a sick society that is far from God."[36]

An early example of the subtle, transformative, healing affect the Church has on the world is how the Church by the witness of her community life helped to bring about the end of slavery. With respect to slavery and other similar evil institutions, Lohfink argues, that "[T]he antisocial and corrupt systems of a dominant society cannot be at-

---

[36] Lohfink, *Jesus and Community*, 1709.

tacked more sharply than by the formation of an anti-society in its midst. Simply through its existence, this new society is a much more efficacious attack on the old structures than any programs, without personal cost, for the general transformation of the world."[37] The Church's counter-witness to the practice of slavery included promoting slaves to the high church offices and treating them as equals in Christ, as St. Paul encouraged in his Epistle to Philemon.

Chapter 4 Discussion Questions

1. Compare, in a specific sense, at least three early Church Fathers who are mentioned in Chapter 4 on what distinguishes the Catholic Church from other communities. Do so in at least five different ways. Then relate these distinguishing features to today, for example, by discussing which of these aspects could be emphasized more by members in the Catholic Church of today.

2. Respond to the following from Vonier, "If Christians have been good individually, as a Church they have failed miserably. Such is the modern verdict." Include in your answer the following: Pentecost, Holy Spirit, God as Father, Mystical Body, *corpus mixtum*, pilgrim/militant Church, Heavenly Church, holiness of an individual Catholic, and holiness of the Church as a community.

---

[37] Lohfink, *Jesus and Community*, 1189.

3. Explain how the Church helped to bring an end to slavery. Include the following in your response: social order of the Church, Christian witness as a community, political order of the world, evangelization and missionary activity.

Chapter 5

Priests as Fathers

Introduction

In this chapter, we will apply what we have studied in the previous chapters to Catholic priests, specifically by examining what it means for a priest to be a spiritual father. To conceive the fatherhood of the priesthood correctly its hierarchical context needs to be understood. The origin of the term comes from the Greek *hieros,* meaning sacred, and *arche,* meaning rule, or origin. According to Ratzinger, for the Catholic Church, "[t]he correct translation of this term is probably not 'sacred rule' but 'sacred origin.'"[1] The sacred origin of the priestly spiritual father-

---

[1] Ratzinger, *Salt of the Earth,* trans. Adrian Walker (San Francisco: Ignatius Press, 1997), 190-191. "The correct translation of this term is probably not 'sacred rule' but 'sacred origin'. The word *arche* can mean both things, origin and rule. But the likelier meaning is 'sacred origin'. In other words, it communicates itself in virtue of an origin, and the power of this origin, which is sacred, as it were the ever-new beginning of every generation in the Church. It doesn't live by the mere continuum of generations but by the presence of the ever-new source itself, which communicates itself unceasingly through the sacraments. That, I think, is an important, different way of looking at things: the category that corresponds to the

hood is the Fatherhood of God, encountered through Jesus Christ. This means that the fatherhood of a priest is a participation in the one priesthood of Jesus Christ.

The mission priests have been given is precisely to participate in the mission of Jesus in a collective sense. In defining this mission, He received from His heavenly Father Jesus said, "Just Father, the world has not known you, but I have known you; and these men have known that you sent me. To them I have revealed your name, and will continue to reveal it so that your love for me may live in them, and I may live in them." (John 17:25-26 NAB)

In this chapter, we will study the important need of the world to know and experience the Heavenly Father's love for them that priests are to mediate through the one priesthood of Jesus Christ. First, we will examine this from the perspective of psychology. This will be followed on a section on specific characteristics priests are to assume and grow in.

Fathers Who Harm and Atheism

The Catholic psychologist Paul C. Vitz in *Faith of the Fatherless: The Psychology of Atheism* argues, against Sigmund Freud, that people who have had deficient fathers are more likely to become atheists than people who have had

---

priesthood is not that of rule. On the contrary, the priesthood has to be a conduit and a making present of a beginning and has to make itself available for this task. When priesthood, episcopacy, and papacy are understood essentially in terms of rule, then things are truly wrong and distorted."

Ch. 5: Priests as Fathers

loving, protective fathers, even if these fathers were atheists themselves.

According to Freud, belief in God originated from guilt of ancient cannibals. The guilt of these cannibals originated from sons who in a competitive rage collectively killed their powerful, domineering father who jealously kept all women to himself. After killing their father, the brothers then ate him. This meal, writes Freud, "which is perhaps mankind's first celebration, would be the repetition and commemoration of this memorable, criminal act with which so many things began, social organization, moral restrictions and religion."[2] The guilt of the murdered and cannibalized father was the seed of religion, posed Freud, since even though the tyrannical father who jealously horded women to himself was dead, his memory along with the guilt of murdering and eating their father, lived on in the sons' minds. In time this guilt and memory grew into belief of a transcendent, all powerful, terrifying divine father. In reference to this fantastic explanation for the origin of religion, Vitz points out that this theory of Freud is not supported by data. Vitz writes:

> [T]here is no systematic empirical evidence to support the thesis of childhood projection being the basis of belief in God. Indeed, the assumption that religious belief is neurotic and psychologically counterproduc-

---

[2] Sigmund Freud, "Totem and Taboo," p. 68, http://s-f-walker.org.uk/pubsebooks/pdfs/Sigmund_Freud_Totem_and_Taboo.pdf; Paul C. Vitz, *Faith of the Fatherless: The Psychology of* Atheism (San Francisco: Ignatius Press, 2013, loc. 290.

tive has been substantially rejected. Instead, there is now much research showing that a serious religious life is associated with greater physical health and psychological well-being.[3]

Empirical evidence indicates that instead of a tyrannical father causing belief in a father God, such a deficient father encourages the development of atheism in his children. Vitz demonstrates this by examining the lives of prominent atheists including: Adolf Hitler, Joseph Stalin, and Mao Ze Dong. The fathers of these atheists were physically abusive towards their children. This led the children to hate their human fathers, and in so doing set the children up to later reject God. Other notable atheists, especially Friedrich Nietzsche, rejected God not because their fathers abused their power but rather because their fathers were deficient in another way, deficient by not using their power, for various reasons, to guard, protect and defend their family.

As is evident for Vitz, there are a variety of ways that a father can be deficient and set up his children to reject God including being "absent through death or abandonment," being "obviously weak, cowardly, and unworthy of respect, even if he is otherwise pleasant or 'nice,'" and being present but, at the same time, being "physically, sexually, or psychologically abusive."[4]

Along with deficient nurture, nature, what one is born with, may also be a partial cause of atheism. Vitz demon-

---

[3] Paul C. Vitz, *Faith of the Fatherless: The Psychology of Atheism* (San Francisco: Ignatius Press, 2013), Loc. 256.

[4] Vitz, *Faith of the Fatherless*, Loc. 353.

strates this by examining autism. Autistic people have difficulty, in varying degrees, with relating to others, including with their fathers. Since autistic children lack interpersonal skill, they are less likely to bond with their fathers and thereby experience a father's love. This, in turn, makes these autistic children less likely to believe in a personal, loving God, or even in God at all.[5] According to one study, those who are ranked high on the autism spectrum have a marked tendency to be atheistic or at least lack belief in religion.[6] Not surprisingly, autism affects males three to four times more than females, and for this reason and others, including the association of interpersonal skills as a distinctively feminine strength, is sometimes viewed as a characteristic of a person suffering from a "hyper-male type of brain."[7]

When males who do not suffer from autism are compared with females, research has shown that men have a greater tendency towards atheism than women do. The correlation may be because men are less likely to believe in a God, especially in a personal God, since they are more likely than women to be less sensitive to relationships, including their relationship with their father, which in turn causes them to be less open to a relationship with God.

According to his analysis of data drawn from the 2007

---

[5] Vitz, *Faith of the Fatherless,* Loc. 2233.

[6] Vitz, *Faith of the Fatherless*, Loc. 2223.

[7] Vitz, *Faith of the Fatherless*, Loc. 2223. For an interesting article on pastoral care of autistic children see: Elise Ehrhard, "The Transgender Movement Targets Autistic Children," Dec. 12, 2016, http://crisismagazine.com/2016/autism-transgendered-movement.

Pew Forum Study, Peter Martin demonstrated that men are more likely to be atheistic than females and more likely to believe in God as an abstract, non-personal force rather than as a Person. In his analysis, the male proportion of various approaches to religion are as follows: "Atheist, 70%; Agnostic, 64%; Buddhist, 53%; Muslim, 54%; Catholic, 46%; Total Protestants, 46%."[8] An explanation of the male propensity towards atheism is partly revealed in current research that has shown that women statistically value relationships and emotions more than men, who statistically value logic and objective thinking more than women.[9]

Fathers Who Heal

Ultimately, the Father who brings us healing is God the Father. To experience the healing Fatherhood of God,

---

[8] Vitz, *Faith of the Fatherless,* Loc. 2269.

[9] Vitz, *Faith of the Fatherless,* Loc. 1851. Vitz briefly mentions other factions besides the two discussed in the chapter. These include, "My ultimate interpretation of atheists is that they are the product of their 1. historical period, 2. interpersonal trauma with attachment insecurity (e.g., the defective father) and/or in many cases, interpersonal incompetence (e.g., autistic mental characteristics), 3. above-average intelligence, 4. ambition and resentment and sometimes envy—and last but far from the least— 5. their own free choice. My focus, of course, has been on defective fathers, attachment insecurity with a dismissive attitude, and, to a lesser degree, deficient or limited interpersonal sensitivity, as in autism." Vitz, *Faith of the Fatherless*, Loc. 2384.

Ch. 5: Priests as Fathers

Fr. Larry Richards recommends reflecting on chapter three of Luke:

> Now when all the people were baptized, and when Jesus also had been baptized and was praying, the heaven was opened, and the Holy Spirit descended upon him in bodily form like a dove. And a voice came from heaven, "You are my Son, the Beloved; with you I am well pleased." (Luke 3: 21-22 NRSV)

Since we are God's children through Jesus Christ, the Father's words from heaven to Jesus are also addressed to us. To what extent do we believe that we are the beloved children of our Heavenly Father?[10]

Our beloved status is affirmed throughout Revelation, beginning with Genesis. In chapter one of Genesis after creating aspects of the universe God sees them as "good." (Genesis 1: 3, 9 1218, 21, 24 NAB) Finally, once he creates Adam and Eve, he sees them as "very good." (Genesis 1: 31 NAB) In describing this contemplative gaze of God, the English mystic Julian of Norwich writes, "I see God, sitting at a table, smiling, completely relaxed, his [God's] face like a marvelous symphony."[11] Fr. Ron Rolheiser, in

---

[10] Larry Richards, *Be a Man!* (San Francisco, Ignatius Press, 2009), 42.

[11] Ron Rolheiser, "Smiling God Undermines Our Workaholism," http://ronrolheiser.com/smiling-god-undermines-our-workaholism-101295/#.VzCKdmPXvnh. A similar understanding of God is found in an African catechism which answers the question, "Why did God create us?" with "God created us because he thought we

commenting on this Biblically inspired understanding of God as a loving Father who rejoices in the goodness He created, states:

> Most of us, I suspect, are no longer much haunted by images of a punishing, legalistic, vindictive and arbitrary God, a God who records every sin and who exacts an ounce of suffering for an ounce of sin. Few of us still suffer from this particular fear.
>
> Most of us, however, still suffer form an equally unhealthy and debilitating fear of God. Today this just takes a different form. For us, God is no longer the great watchdog in the sky, but is, nonetheless, far, far from pleased, relaxed and smiling. Our God, instead, is a workaholic, overly-intense, wired, displeased and semi-neurotic.
>
> He no longer threatens us with hellfire, but he isn't smiling, relaxed and pleased either. This is equally true in liberal and conservative circles—both of which mirror, precisely, the neurotic intensity and constant displeasure that come from believing in a hyper, workaholic and unhappy God.[12]

Our misunderstanding God as one who first finds fault, who first sees what is wrong before He sees the

---

would enjoy it. Gregory Carlson, *A Retreat with the Spiritual Exercises: Images, Poems, and Stories* (Now You Know Media).

[12] Rolheiser, "Smiling God Undermines Our Workaholism."

Ch. 5: Priests as Fathers

good, influences how we perceive the world. This misperception of God the Father leads us to see reality in an excessively critical manner. For priests, this may translate into being poor images of God's fatherhood. When we reflect on how Jesus revealed the fatherhood of God we see him repeatedly accent the positive, including the potential for goodness since all while living may convert, and in so doing, actualize their great potential for goodness. In demonstrating from the New Testament this manner of seeing the world, Fr. Menard writes:

> Jesus never said to the Samaritan woman: This woman is fickle, light headed, stupid, she is marked by the moral and religious atavism of her milieu, she is only a woman! He asks her for a glass of water and converses with her. (Jn 4, 1-42).
>
> Jesus never said about Mary Magdala: Here's a public sinner, a prostitute bogged down in sin. He said: She has a better chance for the Kingdom of God than those who are holding on to their riches or who pride themselves in their virtue or knowledge. (Lk 7, 36-49).
>
> Jesus did not say to the woman caught in adultery: This is a prostitute. He said: I do not condemn you. Go and do not sin any more. (Jn 8, 9-10).
>
> Jesus did not say to the woman with a hemorrhage: This person who seeks to touch my garment is nothing but an hysteric. He listens to her, speaks with her and heals her. (Lk 8, 43-48).

Jesus did not say to this old lady who put her offering into the treasury of the Temple that she was superstitious. He said she was extraordinary and that we should imitate her disinterestedness. (Mk 12, 41-44).

Jesus did not say: These children are only kids. He said: Let them come to me and try to resemble them (Mt 19, 13-15).

Jesus did not say: This man, Zacchaeus, is nothing but a crooked tax collector who is taking advantage of those in power and bleeding the poor. He invites himself to his table and obtains for him the salvation of his household. (Lk 19, 1-10).

Jesus did not say to those who were with him: This blind man is paying dearly for his sins or those of his ancestors. He says that they are completely wrong on his account, and surprises everyone, his apostles, the scribes and the pharisees, by showing them how much this man has God's favor: "So that the works of God might be made visible through him" (Jn 9, 1-5).

Jesus did not say: This Roman centurion is an intruder. He said: "Not even in Israel have I found such faith" (Lk 7, 1-10).

Jesus did not say: This learned Nicodemus is an intellectual. He opened his eyes to a spiritual rebirth. (Jn 3, 1-21).

Jesus did not say: Judas is a traitor. He embraces him

and says: My friend. (Mt 26, 50).

Jesus did not say: This boaster is nothing but a renegade. He tells him: Peter, do you love me? (Jn 21, 15-17).

Jesus did not say: These high priests are nothing but iniquitous judges, this king is nothing but a puppet, this roman procurator is nothing but a coward, this crowd that is booing me is nothing but plebs, these soldiers who are mistreating me are nothing but army recruits. He said: "Father, forgive them, for they know not what they are doing" (Lk 23, 24).

Jesus never said: There is nothing good in this one, that one, in this milieu, in that one. In our days, he would never have said: He is nothing but a conservative, a liberal, a fascist, a heathen, a bigot…For him, others, whoever they may be, whatever their actions, their status, their reputation, are always loved by God.

Never has a man respected others like this man. He is unique. He is the only Son of Him who makes his sun rise on the good and the bad. (Mt 5, 48). In each one He encounters, he always sees an extraordinary potential! A brand new future! In spite of the past. In you, could it not be the same? Have you realized that at baptism, you received the same Holy Spirit through whom Jesus operates?[13]

---

[13] Eusebe Menard, *Rule of Life 1987*, 228-229. This is an unpublished manuscript.

Entering more deeply in a life of prayer that is informed by Revelation greatly helps priests to perceive the world more as God the Father sees the world and as Jesus reveals to us how to see the world. May God grant us the gift of a contemplative gaze. For this to occur, though, we need to fast from being, borrowing from Rolheiser, a "workaholic, overly-intense, wired, displeased and semi-neurotic."[14] On this note of fasting from overwork, a wise retreat master once told Fr. Gregory I Carlson, S.J., "Don't just do something, sit there."[15] Essentially what the retreat master was saying is avoid being busy just to fill up time, for to encounter the deepest reality, who is God, we need at times simply to stop working and enter deeply into prayer. In prayer, our restless hearts find their rest, since, as St. Augustine writes in his Confessions, "our hearts are restless till they find rest in Thee."[16]

Carlson relates the workaholic who has an excessively critical gaze with a failure to accept our identity as a "beloved child of God." The less we perceive ourselves and others as, in Christ, beloved children of God, the greater will be the tendency to "strive excessively to impress others" in an ambitious attempt to prove we matter. To prove we matter, that we are important we may even try to make a mark on the world in a violent, non-respectful manner of

---

[14] Ron Rolheiser, "Smiling God Undermines Our Workaholism," http://ronrolheiser.com/smiling-god-undermines-our-workaholism-101295/#.VzCKdmPXvnh.

[15] Gregory Carlson, *A Retreat with the Spiritual Exercises: Images, Poems, and Stories* (Now You Know Media).

[16] Augustine, *The Confessions of Saint Augustine*, trans. J.G. Pilkington (ebook, 1892), book 1, chapter1.

other children of God.

Awareness of our identity as beloved children of God, however, will not come primarily through more and more activity, no matter how noble it is, but rather is received from God as a gift inherent in our very being as good since we are created by a good God and made in His image and likeness.[17] Depending on the father figures in our life who have affected our perception of the Fatherhood of God, some of us may need more grace from God in order to understand His fatherhood correctly, for this to happen, advises Fr. Larry Richards, "You should not limit yourself to your father, your grandfather, your past, or your lineage. Your history in this world does not define you; your salvation history in Christ, Who created you and lives inside of you, defines who you are."[18]

The more we accept our beloved identity in a prayerful, contemplative manner the more likely the good that we do, the virtue we practice, will be motivated by a good intention, the intention of doing everything for the Heavenly Father's glory and not for our glory, not for our affirmation, not for the applause we want to receive from others for having been successful. The less we are aware of our identity as beloved children of God the more we will be prone to what has been described in an Augustinian manner, as splendid vices that are not actually true virtues, but only have the appearance of virtue since they are motivated by praise and honor that we want to receive in this

---

[17] Gregory Carlson, *A Retreat with the Spiritual Exercises: Images, Poems, and Stories* (Now You Know Media).

[18] Larry Richards, *Be a Man!* (San Francisco, Ignatius Press, 2009), 42.

life.[19]

In his book *Behold the Man: A Catholic Vision of Male Spirituality*, Deacon Harold Burke-Sivers identifies important characteristics of men, especially priests, that best allow a fathers to be icons of the Fatherhood of God. These include being vulnerable, obedient, protective guardians of the weak, relational, affectively mature, ethical, and able to move people both emotionally and rationally.[20]

Burke-Sivers defines vulnerability as the ability to "open ourselves fully and share our hearts and souls with others."[21] For a priest this characteristic is essential for we are called to lead and accompany people spiritually, which requires them to relate in a personal manner with others. The characteristic of obedience, of following another's lead and not always insisting on being the leader, comes from Christ, Who was always obedient to His Heavenly Father, and from St. Joseph who even when he did not understand obeyed the heavenly Father. Being protective

---

[19] Philip Cary, *Augustine: Philosopher and Saint*, CDs (Chantilly: The Great Courses, 1997).

[20] "For Aristotle there were three [leadership qualities]: ethos, pathos, and logos. The ethos is his moral character and the source of his ability to convince others [of what is true]; the pathos is his ability to touch feelings and move people emotionally; the logos is his ability to give solid reasons for particular actions and, therefore, to move people intellectually." Harold Burke-Sivers, *Behold the Man: A Catholic Vision of Male Spirituality* (San Francisco: Ignatius Press, 2015), loc. 3071.

[21] Burke-Sivers, *Behold the Man*, loc. 291.

of the weak and vulnerable is a key characteristic applied to God in the Old Testament and evident in Jesus' life. Relationality is essential because God as Triune is a relation of persons. As applied to the priest, a priest is not to be a leader in a generic sense, or in a business sense as a CEO but in a personal manner as father, as husband of the Church his bride, and as a brother to his brother priests and to the people he serves.[22]

The characteristic of affective maturity, along with other related priestly, characteristics, was explained extraordinary well by St. John Paul II in his encyclical letter on the formation of priests titled *Pastores Dabo Vobis*:

> 43. …In order that his ministry may be humanly as credible and acceptable as possible, it is important that the priest should mold his human personality in such a way that it becomes a bridge and not an obstacle for others in their meeting with Jesus Christ the Redeemer of humanity. …
>
> Future priests should therefore cultivate a series of human qualities, not only out of proper and due growth and realization of self, but also with a view to the ministry. These qualities are needed for them to be balanced people, strong and free, capable of bearing the weight of pastoral responsibilities. They need to be educated to love the truth, to be loyal, to respect every person, to have a sense of justice, to be true to their word, to be genuinely compassionate, to be men of in-

---

[22] Burke-Sivers, *Behold the Man: A Catholic Vision of Male Spirituality*, loc. 2479.

tegrity and, especially, to be balanced in judgment and behavior. ...

Of special importance is the capacity to relate to others. This is truly fundamental for a person who is called to be responsible for a community and to be a "man of communion." This demands that the priest not be arrogant, or quarrelsome, but affable, hospitable, sincere in his words and heart, prudent and discreet, generous and ready to serve, capable of opening himself to clear and brotherly relationships and of encouraging the same in others, and quick to understand, forgive and console (125) (cf. 1 Tm. 3:1-5; Ti. 1:7-9). ...

In this context affective maturity, which is the result of an education in true and responsible love, is a significant and decisive factor in the formation of candidates for the priesthood.

44. Affective maturity presupposes an awareness that love has a central role in human life. In fact, as I have written in the encyclical *Redemptor Hominis*, "Man cannot live without love. He remains a being that is incomprehensible for himself; his life is meaningless, if love is not revealed to him, if he does not encounter love, if he does not experience it and make it his own, if he does not participate intimately in it.[23]

---

[23] John Paul II, "Pastores Dabo Vobis,", no. 43-44, March 25, 1992, http://w2.vatican.va/content/john-paul-

Affective maturity, by which one receives love and loves in return in appropriate, non-manipulative ways, is based on what John Paul II titles the "nuptial meaning of the body."[24] It is vital for a priest to view the body and his emotions as gifts from God to be directed in a reasonable and loving manner since, explains John Paul II, "the charism of celibacy, even when it is genuine and has proved itself, leaves one's affections and instinctive impulses intact."[25] Those training to be priests, consequently, "need an affective maturity which is prudent, able to renounce anything that is a threat to it, vigilant over both body and spirit, and capable of esteem and respect in interpersonal relationships between men and women."[26]

---

ii/en/apost_exhortations/documents/hf_jp-ii_exh_25031992_pastores-dabo-vobis.html.

[24] Ultimately, only God gives in way that is completely absent from self-interest. In contrast, due to original and personal sin, when we give some aspect of manipulation is present in which the gift-giver tries to subtly influence the receiver of the gift to act in a way that benefits the gift-giver. Robert Barron, "Forgiving Dylann Roof," March 2017, *First Things*, https://www.firstthings.com/article/2017/03/forgiving-dylann-roof#login.

[25] John Paul II, "Pastores Dabo Vobis," no. 44, March 25, 1992, http://w2.vatican.va/content/john-paul-ii/en/apost_exhortations/documents/hf_jp-ii_exh_25031992_pastores-dabo-vobis.html.

[26] John Paul II, "Pastores Dabo Vobis," no. 44, March 25, 1992, http://w2.vatican.va/content/john-paul-ii/en/apost_exhortations/documents/hf_jp-ii_exh_25031992_pastores-dabo-vobis.html.

Chapter 5 Discussion Questions

1. How may the two ways of defining Catholic hierarchy explained by Ratzinger influence a priest's understanding of priesthood, pope, bishop, and laity? In answering provide two fictional examples that illustrate these two different ways of perceiving Catholic hierarchy.

2. Contrast Freud's erroneous explanation for belief in God with Paul C. Vitz's explanation for atheism. Include the following in your response: jealous father, women, envious sons, patricide, guilt, Hitler (or another dictator), Nietzsche, autism, men and atheism.

3. Discuss how encountering the Fatherhood of God heals us from what has been called the "father wound" from deficient father figures. Include the following in your answer: Genesis 1, Luke 3: 21-22, one or more of the following New Testament passages, Jn 4:1-42, Lk 7:36-49, Jn. 8: 9-10, Lk 8: 43-48, Mk 12:41-44, Mt 19:13-15, Lk 19: 1-10, Jn. 9:1-5, Lk 7: 1-10, Jn. 3:1-21, Mt 26:50, Jn. 21:15-17, Lk 23:24, Mt 5: 48, workaholic, critical gaze, and beloved.

4. In your own words, explain how at least five of the following priestly characteristics help a priest to be effective icons of the God the Father: truthful, loyal, being vulnerable, obedient, protective guardians of the weak, relational, affectively mature, ethical, and able to move people both emotionally and rationally.

Chapter 6

Priests as Brothers

Introduction

As disciples of Jesus with God as Our Father, priests are called to develop fraternal bonds with another. These fraternal bonds are an integral part of being a disciple of Jesus since, Lohfink writes, "Jesus did indeed demand of his disciples that they leave everything, thing, but he did not call them into solitude and isolation. That is not the point of discipleship. He called them into a new family of brothers and sisters, itself a sign of the arriving kingdom."[1] By their celibacy, obedience and, in varying degrees, poverty, priests are called to witness in an intense manner to a fraternal unity that transcends national boundaries. When they do so, the fraternal bonds they form not only help to unite the People of God in the Catholic Church but also strengthen priests to persevere in their vocations.

Priests as Signs of Heavenly Fraternity

A way that priestly fraternity manifests the heavenly kingdom is the priestly commitment to non-violence after the example of Jesus who did not take life but rather gave

---

[1] Gerhard Lohfink, *Jesus and Community: The Social Dimension of Christian Faith*, trans. John P. Galvin (Philadelphia: Fortress Press, 1984), 522.

his life. It is important to note that this is not required in the same way for all disciples of Jesus. In a similar way that not all are called to celibacy, which is a sign of the heavenly kingdom to come, not everyone, especially those in the military, are called to forgo engaging in warfare. Priests, though, are to forgo actively fighting in wars.[2] For this reason, from the early days of Christian history, Church Councils have explicitly prohibited priests from taking up arms.[3] This tradition is reflected in the 1983 Code of Can-

---

[2] Father Barron, now Bishop Barron, once asked Cardinal George on the legitimacy of passivism. Cardinal George said that the Church needs pacifists in a similar way that she needs celibates. Both the pacifist and the celibate witness to way we are called to live in heaven where there will be no violent competition and no physical marriages. Cardinal George then added, "I love celibates, I'm a celibate but I don't want everyone to be a celibate." He also applied this logic to pacifism, especially in light of the Just War Theory. Barron explains it is not prudent, in this fallen sinful world, for police officers not to be violent, or political leaders like Abraham Lincoln who witness fundamental rights being violated. A person does not stage a non-violent protest when he sees someone being assaulted. Due to our fallen state we can't universalize non-violent principles. However, in line with Cardinal George, we are to affirm these principles and affirm those called to witness to passivism without wanting, or expecting, everyone to be a pacifist. Robert Barron, "Bishop Barron on Daniel Berrigan and Non-violence," https://youtu.be/Y-0z2m_NtS8.

[3] Edward Westermarck, *Christianity and Morals* (Oxon:

Routledge, 2013), 217. "One of the Apostolic Canons requires that any bishop, priest, or deacon who devotes himself to military service shall be degraded from his ecclesiastical rank (*Canones ecclesiastici qui dicuntur Apostolorum*, 83 [74] [C.J. Bunsen, *Analecta Ante-Nicaena*, ii, London, 1854, p. 31]). The Councils of Toulouse, in 633 (ch. 45, in Labbe-Mansi, x. 630), and of Meaux, in 845 (can. 37, *ibid*, xiv. 827), condemned to a similar punishment those of the clergy who ventured to take up arms. Gratian says (*Decretum*, ii. 23. 8. 4) that the Church refuses to pray for the soul of a priest who died on the battle-field. But notwithstanding the canons of the Councils and the decrees of the popes, ecclesiastics frequently participated in battles (Nicolaus I., *Epistolae et Decreta*, 83 [Migne, cxix. 922]; W. Robertson, *The History of the Emperor Charles V.*, i [London, 1806], pp. 330, 385; R. Ward, *An Enquiry into the Foundation and History of the Law of Nations in Europe, from the Time of the Greeks and Romans, to the Age of Grotius*, I [London, 1795], p. 365.; H.T. Buckle, *History of Civilization in England* [London, 1894], i. 204, ii. 464; J.F. Bethune-Baker, *The Influence of Christianity on War* [Cambridge, 1888] p. 52; E. Dummler, *Geschichte des Ostfrankischen Reichs* [Berlin and Leipzig, 1862-88], ii. 637). H. Grotius, *De jure belli et pacis*, i. 2. 10. 10; J. Bingham, *Antiquities of the Christian Church*, iv. 4. 1 (Works, ii. [Oxford, 1855], p. 55. *Paenitentiale Bigotianum*, iv. i. 4..." Westermarck points out that the early Church indiscriminately condemned all warfare. Justin Martyr did so in reference to Isaiah: 2, 4). See Justin Martyr *Apologia I*, 39, Tertullian, *De corona*, 11, Origen, *Contra Celsum*, v. 33, viii. 78, Lactantius, *Divinae institutions*, vi ('De vero cultu'), 20, and Tertullian, *Apologeticus*, 42. After the edict of Milan the

on Law specifically in numbers 285, 287, 289:

> Can. 285 – 1. Clerics are to shun completely everything that is unbecoming to their state, in accordance with the provisions of particular law. 2. Clerics are to avoid whatever is foreign to their state, even when it is not unseemly. ... Can. 289 1. As military service ill befits the clerical state, clerics and candidates for sacred orders are not to volunteer for the armed services without permission of their Ordinary.[4]

The 1983 Canon 285 corresponds to Canon 138 of the 1917 code which was a bit more specific:

> Clerics shall entirely abstain from all those things that are indecent to their state; they shall not engage in indecorous arts; they shall abstain from gambling games with risks of money; they shall not carry arms, except when there is just cause for fearing; hunting should not be indulged and [then] never with clamor; taverns and similar places should not be entered without necessity or another just cause approved by the local Or-

---

Church developed her understanding of warfare which lead to the just war theory present in its nascent state in Saint Augustine's thought in *The City of God* and developed by Thomas Aquinas.

[4] E. Caparros, and M. Theriault, *Code of Canon Law Annotated* (Montreal: Wilson & Lafleur Limitee: 1993), 236-239.

dinary.⁵

The reason for the 1983 Canon 285, which is in continuity with 1917 Canon 138, is that, Caparros and Theriault comment, "the priest sets himself up as a symbol and instrument of unity and fraternity amongst all people."⁶ Gerard Sheehy and his fellow editors further explain, "While retaining the general principles of the 1917 Code, the present law does not give details of what might be unbecoming to the clerical state. Since this can vary with time and place, it is left to local legislation to specify what such activities might be. Even without such legislation, any form of criminal or immoral activity is obviously forbidden. Also, clearly unbecoming for a cleric would be such occupations as executioner, bodyguard etc."⁷

Another related way that priests are to foster "unity and fraternity among all people"⁸ is, states the 1983 Canon 285, not "to assume public office whenever it means sharing in the exercise of civil power." The reason the Canon provides is that "Clerics are always to do their utmost to foster among peace and harmony based on justice." Therefore, "[t]hey [clerics] are not to play an active role in politi-

---

⁵ Edward N. Peters, *The 1917 Pio-Benedictine Code of Canon Law* (San Francisco: Ignatius Press, 2001), 70.

⁶ Caparros, and Theriault, *Code of Canon Law Annotated*, 237.

⁷ Gerard Sheehy, Ralph Brown, Donal Kelly, Aidan McGrath, *A Practical Guide to the Code of Canon Law* (Collegeville: The Liturgical Press, 1995), 163.

⁸ Caparros, and Theriault, *Code of Canon Law Annotated*, 237.

cal parties."[9] This fraternal peace and harmony is, explain Caparros and Theriault, to transcend "any ideological and political confrontation. Under no circumstance is it proper for the priest to be a political leader or an official with secular authority."[10]

A notable example of priests being corrected for directly engaging in politics occurred during John Paul II's 1983 visit to Nicaragua. There, he publicly corrected Fr. Ernesto Cardenal for having assumed a political office in the Sandinista government. Since Ernesto refused to step down from his political office, he was suspended from active ministry.[11] Another example involves the Catholic bishop Fernando Lugo Mendez of Paraguay. In April, 2008, he was elected the president of Paraguay. Benedict XVI responded by laicizing the bishop. The reason Paraguay's apostolic nuncio gave for the laicization was that Mendez's "clerical status is incompatible with serving as president."[12]

When priests and bishops directly engage in warfare and/or politics, they obscure their calling to be signs of another family of which we all are called to be brothers and sisters of regardless of our political or national allegiances. This family has God as Our Father and the

---

[9] Ibid., 236-239.

[10] Ibid., 237.

[11] Cathy Caridi, "Can Priests Hold Public Office?" http://canonlawmadeeasy.com/2012/09/20/can-priests-hold-public-office-2/.

[12] "Paraguay's president, ex-bishop, granted lay status July 30, 2008," http://www.catholicculture.org/news/features/index.cfm?recnum=59958.

Church, embodied in Mary, as our mother. In his book *The Meaning of Christian Brotherhood*, Ratzinger encourages us to rediscover this ancient appreciation of Christian brotherhood as a reality in which all are called to participate.

Although the relational term brother, and similar terms, were frequently used when referring to all Catholics in the first centuries of the Church, and even when referring to persecutors of Catholics, in time this relational terminology began to be almost exclusively used among the clergy. The exception to this was the use of the terms brother and sister in monastic and other forms of religious life. This restriction, explains Ratzinger, "of the idea of brotherhood to the hierarchy and to ascetics … has persisted up to our own times, with all its inevitably damaging effects."[13] Keeping in mind Ratzinger's desire for all in the

---

[13] "By the third century, however, the word "brother" is found less and less as a designation among Christians. It is instructive for an understanding of the inner development of the Church to see the two ways in which the word finally comes to be used. The first usage we find in Cyprian who no longer employs the word "brother" as a term of address to Christians, except to bishops and clerics. This is no longer the old brotherhood of the faithful; it reminds one rather of the well-known secular idea of the brotherhood of princes with each other which was later to become clearly apparent in the gradations of address for bishops, presbyters, and laymen. The other usage developed in the context of asceticism, in the monastic communities, in which the idea of 'brother' and 'sister' lived on after it had passed away from a Church which had grown too vast for it to have any concrete meaning. Thus there is

Church to recognize all as brothers and sisters of one common Father and mother, we now turn to the need for priests to recognize other priests as their spiritual brothers.

Priestly Fraternity

In the words of John Paul II, a priest is to be a "man of communion."[14] This communion is greatly facilitated when priests foster fraternal relations among one another. The ultimate reason for this distinctly priestly characteristic is, in the words of John Paul II, "the image of the bonds of fraternal affection which Christ himself lived on earth (cf. Jn. 11:5)."[15] The fraternal affection Jesus had for others is captured in one of his titles, Son of Man. St. Irenaeus explains this title in a fraternal manner, by which Christ is the Son of Man, our brother, since he is "the one who renews in himself that first man from whom the race born of

---

a restriction of the idea of brotherhood to the hierarchy and to ascetics, to which actual church life had now become reduced. As we know, this state of affairs has persisted up to our own times, with all its inevitably damaging effects. Thus historical analysis has led to the point from which our reflection about the Christian idea of brotherhood today—its significance and its possibilities—must start." Joseph Ratzinger, *The Meaning of Christian Brotherhood*, (San Francisco: Ignatius Press, 1993), 39-40.

[14] John Paul II, "Pastores Dabo Vobis,", no. 18, March 25, 1992, http://w2.vatican.va/content/john-paul-ii/en/apost_exhortations/documents/hf_jp-ii_exh_25031992_pastores-dabo-vobis.html.

[15] Ibid., no. 43.

woman was formed; as by a man's defeat our race fell into the bondage of death, so by a man's victory we were to rise again to life."[16] Jesus was able "to renew in himself" Adam's sin because He is divine. In the Old Testament, the Son of Man is used both to refer to a man as distinct from God (Psalm 8: 4-5) and as a divine being (Daniel 7: 13-14 RSV). When naming Himself the Son of Man, Jesus refers to this passage from Daniel which describes a "son of man" who will come "with the clouds of heaven" to judge the nations. (Matthew 24:30-31; Luke 17:22-30).[17]

Stephen J. Rossetti in *A Study of the Psychological and Spiritual Health of Priests* convincingly demonstrates that when a priest is a man of communion, and, consequently, has priest brothers upon whom he can rely, he is much more likely to be healthy and happy and to persevere. Rossetti writes:

For a priest to connect and be part of the presbyterate

---

[16] St. Irenaeus, "From a Treatise Against Heresies, book 5, 19," *Liturgy of the Hours*, Volume 1 (New York: Catholic Book Publishing Company, 1975), 244.

[17] Jodi Magness, *Jesus and His Jewish Influences*, Course Transcript (Chantilly: The Great Courses, 2015), 176-178. "That is why the Lord proclaims himself the Son of Man, the one who renews in himself that first man from whom the race born of woman was formed; as by a man's defeat our race fell into the bondage of death, so by a man's victory we were to rise again to life." St. Irenaeus, "From a Treatise Against Heresies, book 5, 19," *Liturgy of the Hours*, Volume 1 (New York: Catholic Book Publishing Company, 1975), 244.

is not something peripheral to the priesthood. The priest is ordained into a community, and an essential part of his spiritual life is this sacramental bond he shares with his bishop and brother priests. Nurturing these relationships nurtures his own priesthood and contributes significantly to his overall spiritual life.[18]

Rossetti's study revealed that a great danger to fraternal life among priests is overwork. His data demonstrates that priests who overwork are much less likely to have friends on whom they can rely since they did not foster these relationships. Priests who lack a supportive network of friends are also less likely to take a day off for relaxation which causes them to further overwork and to be dangerously isolated.[19] A risk, among others, of over-work is burnout. According to Rossetti's statistics, younger priests have the highest rate of burnout. These young priests, writes Rossetti, "are less comfortable in their human relationships than the older priests as they learn how to develop good pastoral relationships without crossing dangerous boundaries."[20]

Rossetti's work with priests who have crossed over dangerous boundaries convinced him that there is a direct relationship between developing interpersonal relationships with other and deepen-ing a relationship with God. In reference to the Gospel of Matthew (22:37-39), Rossetti

---

[18]Stephen J. Rossetti, *A Study of the Psychological and Spiritual Health of Priests* (Notre Dame: Ave Maria Press, 2011), Loc. 283.

[19] Ibid., Loc. 421.

[20] Ibid., Loc. 893.

writes, "We are made in the image of God. So, if people cannot love the 'God images' in front of them, how can they love the fullness of God? Coming to love the 'God images' in front of us leads directly to loving God more. The New Testament says this. My experience with priest in treatment has supported this. The current study underscores this truth."[21]

A common obstacle that some priests face that prevents them from developing interpersonal relationships Rossetti found is anger, but not anger that is a "passing emotion we feel at injustice,"[22] which Jesus also experienced and is described in the New Testament, for example when He cleansed the Temple (Matthew 21:12-13).[23] The anger that is an obstacle to communion which Jesus completely lacked is, writes Rossetti, "a deep-seated anger that

---

[21] Ibid., Loc. 1644.

[22] Ibid., Loc. 1662.

[23] Also see Matthew 16:23 when Jesus rebukes Peter for having tried to dissuade Him from the cross, Matthew 23 when Jesus chastises the scribes and Pharisees, Mark 1: 23-28 when Jesus rebukes a demon possessing a man, Mark 3:5 when Jesus becomes angry at Pharisees who do not want him to heal a man with a withered hand, Mark 10:14 when Jesus became indignant when his disciples shooed away children from Him, Matthew 21:12-17 when Jesus cleansed the temple. In some of these examples, Jesus' anger can be explained as a reaction to people trying to exclude others from salvation under the cover of being a chosen people, or being chosen by Jesus.

sticks in their souls and eats away at them."[24] Priests who respond to the following statements in the affirmative, according to Rossetti, very likely suffer from this "deep-seated anger" that prevents them from being an authentic man of communion that we are called to be. The questions are as follows: "I have consistent problems getting along with people"; "I have trouble managing my anger"; "My relationships seem to have more conflict than others have"; and "I have angry outbursts which upset others."[25] Rossetti comments:

> [D]amaging one's relationships with others results in damage to one's relationship with God. Heaven - where God "lives," or rather we should say, where God is - is a place of communion and peace. Hell, on the other hand, is a place of isolation and rage where there are no deep human connections and no inner peace. It is a place consumed with rage. We see the dynamics of heaven and hell being played out in this statistical study of the lives of priests. Those who find inner peace and communion, move closer to God. Actually, the fact that they find this inner peace and communion means ipso facto that they are connecting with God. But when they fall into isolation and anger, they are drifting into hell.[26]

As supported by Rossetti's data, obstacles to commun-

---

[24] Rossetti, *A Study of the Psychological and Spiritual Health of Priests*, Loc. 1662.
[25] Ibid.
[26] Ibid., Loc. 1668.

ion with God and with our brothers and sisters can be healed or prevented from occurring by beginning and maintaining healthy friendships[27] including being community leaders,[28] attending priestly gatherings, Marian devo-

---

[27] One principle that some may find helpful to follow which can make sure friendships remain healthy and not opportunities to criticize others to the detriment of community life was taught to me from a priest who once was a Christian Brother. When he was a brother, the Christian Brothers followed the principle "rarely one, never two, always three". This phrase indicates that a Christian Brother should rarely go out by himself, never go out with just one brother, and always go out with two or more brothers.

[28] In their work *Evolving Visions of the Priesthood* Hoge and Wenger distinguished cultic priests who locate their identity in prayer, and the sacraments from pastoral priests who locate their identity in being pastorally sensitive and community leaders and coordinators. Rossetti points out that, as with many realities in the Church, a priest is called by his vocation to be cultic and pastoral, prayerful, sacramentally centered and pastorally sensitive community leaders. Stephen J. Rossetti, *A Study of the Psychological and Spiritual Health of Priests* (Notre Dame: Ave Maria Press, 2011), Loc. 1668. Burke-Sivers also disagrees with "such a dichotomy for two main reasons. First, one does not find this manner of discourse in Vatican II or elsewhere in the Church's teaching. Second, the attempt to contrast 'cultic' and 'pastoral' presupposes wrongly that the three-fold munera of the priest (teaching, sanctifying, and governing) are somehow in competition with each other, or are exclusive of each other. The Church instead takes a wider view.

tion, regularly praying the Liturgy of the Hours, a daily holy hour and frequenting the Sacrament of Reconciliation.[29] One additional factor that fosters a healthy life is practicing the virtue of *eutrapelia*, which Aquinas includes in his *Summa Theologica* and borrowed from the Greek tradition, specifically from Aristotle. *Eutrapelia* roughly translates as the virtue of play which stands between being a boor and being a clown.[30]

Such a solution does not reach deep enough. The problem is not 'cultic' priests or 'pastoral' priests, but humanly relational priests as men, as husbands and as fathers." Burke-Sivers, *Behold the Man*, loc. 2390.

[29] Rossetti, *A Study of the Psychological and Spiritual Health of Priests*, Loc. 1400, 1714, 1783, 1813, 1841, 1904.

[30] "Just as man needs bodily rest for the body's refreshment, because he cannot always be at work, since his power is finite and equal to a certain fixed amount of labor, so too is it with his soul, whose power is also finite and equal to a fixed amount of work. Consequently when he goes beyond his measure in a certain work, he is oppressed and becomes weary, and all the more since when the soul works, the body is at work likewise, in so far as the intellective soul employs forces that operate through bodily organs. Now sensible goods are connatural to man, and therefore, when the soul arises above sensibles, through being intent on the operations of reason, there results in consequence a certain weariness of soul, whether the operations with which it is occupied be those of the practical or of the speculative reason. Yet this weariness is greater if the soul be occupied with the work of contemplation, since thereby it is raised higher above sensible

things; although perhaps certain outward works of the practical reason entail a greater bodily labor. On either case, however, one man is more soul-wearied than another, according as he is more intensely occupied with works of reason. Now just as weariness of the body is dispelled by resting the body, so weariness of the soul must needs be remedied by resting the soul: and the soul's rest is pleasure, as stated above (I-II:25:2; I-II:31:1 ad 2). Consequently, the remedy for weariness of soul must needs consist in the application of some pleasure, by slackening the tension of the reason's study. Thus in the Conferences of the Fathers xxiv, 21, it is related of Blessed John the Evangelist, that when some people were scandalized on finding him playing together with his disciples, he is said to have told one of them who carried a bow to shoot an arrow. And when the latter had done this several times, he asked him whether he could do it indefinitely, and the man answered that if he continued doing it, the bow would break. Whence the Blessed John drew the inference that in like manner man's mind would break if its tension were never relaxed.

Now such like words or deeds wherein nothing further is sought than the soul's delight, are called playful or humorous. Hence it is necessary at times to make use of them, in order to give rest, as it were, to the soul. This is in agreement with the statement of the Philosopher (Ethic. iv, 8) that "in the intercourse of this life there is a kind of rest that is associated with games": and consequently it is sometimes necessary to make use of such things.

Nevertheless it would seem that in this matter there are three points which require especial caution. The first and chief is that the pleasure in question should not be

Chapter 6 Discussion Questions

1. How are priests to be signs of heavenly fraternity? Include the following in your answer: warfare, di-

---

sought in indecent or injurious deeds or words. Wherefore Tully says (De Offic. i, 29) that "one kind of joke is discourteous, insolent, scandalous, obscene." Another thing to be observed is that one lose not the balance of one's mind altogether. Hence Ambrose says (De Offic. i, 20): "We should beware lest, when we seek relaxation of mind, we destroy all that harmony which is the concord of good works": and Tully says (De Offic. i, 29), that, "just as we do not allow children to enjoy absolute freedom in their games, but only that which is consistent with good behavior, so our very fun should reflect something of an upright mind." Thirdly, we must be careful, as in all other human actions, to conform ourselves to persons, time, and place, and take due account of other circumstances, so that our fun "befit the hour and the man," as Tully says (De Offic. i, 29).

Now these things are directed according to the rule of reason: and a habit that operates according to reason is virtue. Therefore there can be a virtue about games. The Philosopher gives it the name of wittiness (eutrapelia), and a man is said to be pleasant through having a happy turn of mind, whereby he gives his words and deeds a cheerful turn: and inasmuch as this virtue restrains a man from immoderate fun, it is comprised under modesty. [Eutrapelia is derived from trepein = 'to turn']." Thomas Aquinas, "Summa Theologica," II-II, Q. 168, art. 2, newadvent.org, http://www.newadvent.org/ summa/3168.htm#article2,.

rect engagement in politics, fraternity in the Church hierarchy, fraternity in the entire Church, and fraternity outside the Church.

2. Discuss the various ways a priest is to be a man of communion. Include the following in your response: cultic, pastoral, teaching, sanctifying, governing, overwork, friendship, attend-ing priestly gatherings, Marian devotion, regularly praying the Liturgy of the Hours, a daily holy hour, *eutrapelia*, and frequenting the Sacrament of Reconciliation.

Chapter 7

Divine Love in Paganism

Introduction

In the following six chapters, we will shift our attention from God as Father to God as a divine lover, and Revelation as, in the words of Scott Hahn, "a long love letter from the Father to his beloved children still on their earthly pilgrimage."[1] We will begin by situating Revelation within the surrounding pagan context, first by looking at Greek and Roman mythology on divine love, and then by examining the Greek philosophical understanding of love that influenced the early Church.

Divine Love in Mythology

In Greek and Roman mythology, divine love is portrayed as irrational, unreliable and inconstant. This becomes evident when Greek and Roman mythology is examined from the perspective of love among the gods.

The Greek God of love is Eros (Cupid for the Romans). In describing Eros's fickle nature one poem states:

Evil his heart, but honey-sweet his tongue,

---

[1] Scott Hahn, *God's Covenant Love in Scripture: A Father Who Keeps His Promises* (Cincinnati: St. Anthony Messenger Press, 1998), 20.

No truth in him, the rogue. He is cruel in his play.
Small are his hands, yet his arrows fly far as death.
Tiny his shaft, but it carries heaven-high,
Touch not his treacherous gifts, they are dipped in fire.[2]

Frequently, this god of beauty and fertility is portrayed as blindfolded to signify his irrational nature. An early reference to Eros is in Hesiod's *Theogony* (c. 700 BC). Here, Eros is depicted as the most beautiful of Gods and the offspring of Chaos and Gaia, the mother earth goddess. Chaos, explains the *Theogony*, is the disorder that pre-existed the Gods. Out of Chaos came the earth goddess (Gaia), the God of the abyss or underworld (Tartaros), and the God of love (Eros).[3] In other works, Eros is presented

---

[2] Edith Hamilton, *Mythology* (New York: Little, Brown and Company, 1969), 34. For poems on Eros see Anacreon (520 BC). David Sacks, *Encyclopedia of the Ancient Greek World* (New York: Facts on File, 2005), 126.

[3] Hesiod, "Theogony," 104, Perseus Digital Library, http://www.perseus.tufts.edu/hopper/text?doc=Perseus %3Atext%3A1999.01.0130%3Acard%3D104. The following source is cited. Hesiod. The Homeric Hymns and Homerica with an English Translation by Hugh G. Evelyn-White. Theogony. Cambridge, MA. Harvard University Press; London, William Heinemann Ltd. 1914. "Hail, children of Zeus! Grant lovely song and celebrate the holy race of the deathless gods who are forever, those that were born of Earth and starry Heaven and gloomy Night and them that briny Sea did rear. Tell how at the first gods and earth came to be, and rivers, and the boundless sea with its

as a son of Aphrodite, the goddess of love. Close associ-

---

raging swell, and the gleaming stars, and the wide heaven above, and the gods who were born of them, givers of good things, and how they divided their wealth, and how they shared their honors amongst them, and also how at the first they took many-folded Olympus. These things declare to me from the beginning, you Muses who dwell in the house of Olympus, and tell me which of them first came to be. In truth at first Chaos came to be, but next wide-bosomed Earth, the ever-sure foundation of all the deathless ones who hold the peaks of snowy Olympus, and dim Tartarus in the depth of the wide-pathed Earth [Gaia], and Eros (Love), fairest among the deathless gods, who unnerves the limbs and overcomes the mind and wise counsels of all gods and all men within them. From Chaos came forth Erebus [darkness] and black Night [Nyx]; but of Night were born Aether [upper air] and Day [Hemera], whom she conceived and bore from union in love with Erebus. And Earth first bore starry Heaven [Uranus], equal to herself, to cover her on every side, and to be an ever-sure abiding-place for the blessed gods. And she brought forth long hills, graceful haunts of the goddess Nymphs who dwell amongst the glens of the hills. She bore also the fruitless deep with his raging swell, Pontus, [sea] without sweet union of love. But afterwards she lay with Heaven and bore deep-swirling Oceanus, Coeus and Crius and Hyperion and Iapetus, Theia and Rhea, Themis and Mnemosyne and gold-crowned Phoebe and lovely Tethys. After them was born Cronos the wily, youngest and most terrible of her children, and he hated his lusty sire."

ates of Eros include Anteros (god of mutual love), Pothos (god of longing), Hymen ("God of the Wedding Feast"[4]), Himeros (god of desire), Peitho (god of persuasion), the Graces, and the Muses.[5]

The Graces are Aglaia (goddess of splendor), Euphrosyne (goddess of mirth), and Thalia (goddess of Good Cheer). The nine Muses are goddesses of song. These include Clio (goddess of history), Urania (goddess of astronomy), Melpomene (goddess of tragedy), Thalia (goddess of comedy), Terpischore (goddess of dance), Caliope (goddess of epic poetry), Erato (goddess of love-poetry), Polyhymnia (goddess of songs to gods), and Euterpe (goddess of lyric poetry).[6] According to Hesiod, the Muses once revealed to him that, "We know how to speak false things that seem true, but we know, when we will, to utter true things."[7]

The female counterpart to Eros is Aphrodite who, as mentioned previously, in some works is identified as Eros's mother. In the *Theogony*, Aphrodite's origin is traced to the foam of Uranus's castrated sexual organs which were cast into the sea by Uranus's son, Cronus, who was asked by his mother Gaia to castrate his father. Cronus cut off his father's organs with a sickle as his father "lay about Earth [Gaia] spreading himself full upon her."[8] Aphrodite,

---

[4] Hamilton, *Mythology*, 34.

[5] David Sacks, *Encyclopedia of the Ancient Greek World* (New York: Facts on File, 2005), 126.

[6] Hamilton, *Mythology*, 35-36.

[7] Ibid., 36.

[8] Hesiod, "Theogony," 173. The following source is cited. Hesiod. The Homeric Hymns and Homerica with an

the goddess of love and beauty, was born from a violent act done by a son on his father. She is described as having an extraordinary ability to bend others to her manipulative will through her beauty and laughter.[9]

Aphrodite manifested her manipulative ability in events that led to the Trojan War, during which the Greeks defeated the Trojans. This at least semi-mythic war took place between the Trojans and the Greeks after a Trojan, Paris, took for himself Helen, Queen of Sparta, and wife of the king of Sparta, Menelaus. Instead of resolutely resisting Paris' advances on her, Helen fell in love with Paris and then committed adultery with him. Prior to this adulterous act, Aphrodite had promised Paris she would cause Helen to fall in love with him. This was because Paris, chosen by Zeus, had selected Aphrodite as the most beautiful of goddess in a beauty contest set up by Eris, the goddess of strife. In exchange for having been selected and having received from Paris a golden apple symbolizing her unsurpassable beauty, Aphrodite promises and instructs Paris by saying:

> You will set out for Greece on a tour of inspection: and when you get to Sparta, Helen will see you; and for the rest—her falling in love, and going back with you—that will be my affair.... Love and Desire. They shall be your guides. Love will assail her in all his might, and compel her to love you: Desire will en-

---

English Translation by Hugh G. Evelyn-White. Theogony. Cambridge, MA. Harvard University Press; London, William Heinemann Ltd. 1914.

[9] Hamilton, *Mythology*, 29, 51.

compass you about, and make you desirable and lovely as himself; and I will be there to help. I can get the Graces to come too, and between us we shall prevail.[10]

Although Aphrodite kept her promise to Paris, her manipulation of people's hearts ended in disaster for Paris and for other Trojans, many whom were forced to flee from their defeated, burning city. One famous Trojan warrior was Aeneas. Aeneas fled his beloved city to Italian shores with his father Anchises. According to myth, Aeneas was a son of Aphrodite (Venus for the Romans), the mythical founder of the Romans, and the reputed ancestor of Romulus and Remus.[11]

The above descriptions of divine love present in Greek mythology are but a few examples of how the Greeks, and the Romans, exalted sexual love. This exaltation was informed and intertwined with the exaltation of fertility. For example, the Greeks and Romans practiced fertility rites in honor of the gods and goddesses of love.

---

[10] Lucian, "The Dialogues of the Gods," Sacred Texts, http://www.sacred-texts.com/cla/luc/wl1/wl127.htm; Stasinus of Cyprus, "The Epic Cycle," trans. Gregory Nagy, University of Houston, http://www.uh.edu/~cldue/texts/epiccycle.html.

[11] Virgil "Aeneid," Perseus Digital Library, http://www.perseus.tufts.edu/hopper/text?doc=Perseus%3Atext%3A1999.02.0054%3Abook%3D1%3Acard%3D1. The following source is cited. Virgil, *Aeneid*, trans. Theodore C. Williams, (Boston: Houghton Mifflin Co., 1910); Edith Hamilton, *Mythology* (New York: Little, Brown and Company, 1969), 321.

The modern exaltation of sexual love is very different since, as pointed out by G.K. Chesterton, in modernity sexual love is typically not connected with fertility but is considered an end itself. Chesterton argues that, unlike the old paganism's exaltation of sexual love with its association to the natural end of fertility, the new paganism does not lead anywhere since it is disassociated from fertility and ends in lust. Chesterton also held that ancient paganism, such as of the Greeks and Romans, is much more open to being led to Christianity since its understanding of sexual love leads at least to a natural end and by having an end beyond itself could be more easily ordered, and redirected to a supernatural end unlike lust in new paganism which often leads nowhere since it lacks even the natural end of fertility.[12]

Love in Greek Philosophy

The Greeks not only personified love in a multifaceted way in their mythology, but they also theorized about love by distinguishing various loves from one another. Since their explanation of different kinds of love influenced early Christianity, we will end this chapter by examining various forms of love which were identified by the ancient Greeks including *eros*, *storge*, *philia*, and *agape*.

Eros, named after the God Eros, is sexual, desirous

---

[12] Gilbert Keith Chesterton, *The Collected Works of G.K. Chesterton*, Volume 3 (San Francisco: Ignatius Press, 1990), 473, 501-502.

love.[13] Two related types of love are *pothos* which signifies longing for something which or someone who is absent,[14] and *himeros*, which is a desire, not necessarily sexual, that is "irresistible ... requiring immediate satisfaction."[15] *Eros,* in ancient Greek literature, at times is compared with a disease, being struck by a hammer, being doused, fire, theft, heavy mist, and even with madness.[16] Sappho captures the

---

[13] C.S. Lewis, *The Four Loves* (Boston: Houghton Mifflin Harcourt, 1988), 91-116.

[14] Ed Sander, Chiara Thumiger, Chris Carey, and Nick J. Lowe, *Eros in Ancient Greec*e (Oxford: Oxford University Press, 2013), 253.

[15] Claude Calame, *The Poetics of Eros in Ancient Greece*, trans. Janet Lloyd (Princeton: Princeton University Press, 1992), 32.

[16] "By far the commonest NT words for love are the noun agapē and the verb agapan. We shall deal, first, with the noun. Agapē is not a classical word at all; it is doubtful if there is any classical instance of it. In the Septuagint it is used 14 times of sexual love (e.g. Jer. 2.2.) and twice (e.g. Eccles. 9.1) it is used as the opposite of misos, which means hatred. Agapē has not yet become a great word but there are hints of what is to come. The Book of Wisdom uses it for the love of God (Wisdom 3.9) and for the love of wisdom (Wisdom 6.18). The Letter of Aristeas in talking of beauty says (229) that piety is closely connected with beauty, for 'it is the pre-eminent form of beauty, and its power lies in love (agapē) which is the gift of God'. Philo uses agapē once in its nobler sense. He says that phobos (fear) and agapē (love) are kindred feelings and that both are characteristic of man's feeling towards God. But we

Greek understanding of *eros* poetically with:

> He seems just like the gods in heaven,
> That man who sits across from you and cocks his head
> to listen to your lovely voice and charming laugh-
>   which sets my heart
> aflutter in my breast, for when
> I catch the merest glimpse of you,
> my voice is gone,
> my tongue's congealed, a subtle fire
> runs flickering beneath my frame,
> my see blank, a buzzing noise
> assails my ears,
> my sweat is cold, my body's gripped
> by shivers, my skin's yellower
> than grass, it seems as if I'm
> just an inch from death.
> But all is worth the risk since…[17]

Storge is affection between family members. Plato in *Laws* refers to this love with, "A child loves (*stergein*) and is

---

can only find scattered and rare occurrences of this word agapē, which is to become the very key word of NT ethics. Now we turn to the verb agapan. It occurs oftener in classical Greek than the noun, but it is not very common. It can mean to greet affectionately. It can describe the love of money or of precious stones." Christopher A. Faraone, *Ancient Greek Love Magic* (Cambridge: Harvard University Press, 1999), 44.

[17] Sander, et alia, *Eros in Ancient Greece*, 62.

loved by those who begat him."[18] In describing this type of love, C.S. Lewis writes, "The image we must start with is that of a mother nursing a baby; a bitch or a cat with a basketful of puppies or kittens; all in a squeaking, nuzzling heap together; purrings, lickings, baby-talk, milk, warmth, the smell of young life."[19]

Philia refers to love between friends and was seen by ancient Greeks as distinct from *eros* and not formed by it.[20] In distinguishing this type of love from the previous two, Lewis writes, "Without Eros none of us would have been begotten and without Affection [*storge*] none of us would have been reared; but we can live and breed without Friendship."[21] Since friendship need not be formed by erotic love, it is less possessive and, consequently, explains Lewis, "the least jealous of loves. Two friends delight to be joined by a third, and three by a fourth, if only the newcomer is qualified to become a real friend."[22]

In contrast with the New Testament, where *agape* is the most common term for love, *agape* love was rarely used by ancient Greeks in their writing.[23] When the term *agape*

---

[18] See Laws 754b. William Barclay, *New Testament Words* (Louisville: The Westminster Press, 1974), 18.

[19] Lewis, *The Four Loves*, 91-116.

[20] Christopher A. Faraone, *Ancient Greek Love Magic* (Cambridge: Harvard University Press, 1999), 29.

[21] Lewis, *The Four Loves*, 58.

[22] Ibid., 61.

[23] "By far the commonest NT words for love are the noun agapē and the verb agapan. We shall deal, first, with the noun. Agapē is not a classical word at all; it is doubtful if there is any classical instance of it. In the Septuagint it is

Ch. 7: Divine Love in Paganism

was used, it was distinguished from the warm affection of *philia* by signifying the love a master has for a servant and a benefactor has for those he has helped.[24]

---

used 14 times of sexual love (e.g. Jer. 2.2.) and twice (e.g. Eccles. 9.1) it is used as the opposite of misos, which means hatred. Agapē has not yet become a great word but there are hints of what is to come. The Book of Wisdom uses it for the love of God (Wisdom 3.9) and for the love of wisdom (Wisdom 6.18). The Letter of Aristeas in talking of beauty says (229) that piety is closely connected with beauty, for 'it is the pre-eminent form of beauty, and its power lies in love (agapē) which is the gift of God'. Philo uses agapē once in its nobler sense. He says that phobos (fear) and agapē (love) are kindred feelings and that both are characteristic of man's feeling towards God. But we can only find scattered and rare occurrences of this word agapē, which is to become the very key word of NT ethics. Now we turn to the verb agapan. It occurs oftener in classical Greek than the noun, but it is not very common. It can mean to greet affectionately. It can describe the love of money or of precious stones." William Barclay, *New Testament Words* (Louisville: John Knox Press, 1964), loc. 227.

[24] "It can mean *to greet affectionately*. It can describe the love of money or of precious stones. It can be used being content with some thing or some situation. It is even used once (Plutarch, *Pericles*, 1) to describe a society lady caressing a pet lap-dog. But, the great difference between *philein* and *agapan* in classical Greek is that *agapan* has none of the warmth that characterizes *philein*. There are two good instances of this. Dio Cassius reports Antony's famous speech about Caesar, and he says (44.48). 'You loved

Chapter 7 Discussion Questions

1. Describe six specific ways in which divine love is portrayed in Greek mythology as irrational, and/or unreliable and/or inconstant. Include the following in your response: Chaos, Eros, Cronus, Aphrodite and the Trojan War.

2. Contrast the Greek and Roman exaltation of sexual love with the modern tendency to exalt sexual love. Include the following in your response: lust, fertility and natural end.

3. Distinguish the following types loves from one another: *eros, pothos, himeros, storge, philia* and *agape*

(*philein*) him as a father, and you held him in regard (*agapan*) as a benefactor.' *Philein* describes describes the warm love for a father; *agapan* describes the affectionate gratitude for a benefactor. In the *Memorabilia* Xenophon describes how Aristarchus took a problem to Socrates. Owing to war conditions he has fourteen female relatives, displaced persons, billeted on him. They have nothing to do and, not unnaturally, there is trouble. Socrates advises him to set them to work, gentlefolk or not. Aristarchus does and the situation is solved. 'There were happy instead of gloomy faces; they loved (*philein*) him as a protector; he regarded them with affection (*agapan*) because they were useful'. (Xenophon, Memorabilia 2.7.12). Once again there is a warmth in *philein* which is not in *agapan*." William Barclay, *New Testament Words* (Louisville: The Westminster Press, 1974), 19.

Chapter 8

God as Bridegroom and Israel as Bride

Introduction

Divine love in Revelation is distinctly different from the divine love depicted in mythology. We will study this in two parts, first in the Old Testament and then in the New Testament. In this chapter, we will focus our attention on the Old Testament which describes God as creating out of love, choosing Israel for his bride, and specifies Israel's marital obligations.

Created Out of Love

In contrast with mythology, Revelation teaches that God created man out of love and not to have slaves or playthings. Before seeing these essential differences in the Genesis creation accounts, we will look at how the creation of man is presented in pagan mythology, first in Greek mythology and then in Babylonian mythology. This will allow us to see how different the Genesis account is from these ancient pagan myths.

Greek mythology provides little explanation of how and why the gods created human beings.[1] The few scat-

---

[1] Walter Burkert, *Greek Religions*, trans. Blackwell Publishing Ltd and Harvard University Press (Malden: Blackwell Publishing, 1985), 188.

tered references that do refer to the creation of man conflict with one another. According to one myth, Prometheus and his brother Epimethus created human beings. Another myth describes the gods collectively creating five consecutive races of men out of metal, beginning with gold and ending in iron.[2]

In yet another story, the current race of men are descendants from two stones that Deucalion and Pyrrha cast behind them. Deucalion and Pyrrha were human beings whom Prometheus protected from a great flood caused by Zeus to destroy men of the "Bronze Age." These men were punished for their disrespect of the gods. Because Deucalion and Pyrrha gratefully worshipped the Gods, Zeus did not destroy them when he found out they had survived. As the flood was receding, writes Apollodorus, Deucalion and Pyrrha were told by Zeus to pick up stones and throw them over their heads. These stones turned into human beings.[3]

---

[2] Edith Hamilton, *Mythology* (New York: Little, Brown and Company, 1969), 83-92.

[3] "And Prometheus had a son Deucalion. He reigning in the regions about Pythia, married Pyrrha, the daughter of Epimetheus and Pandora, the first woman fashioned by the gods. And when Zeus would destroy the men of the Bronze Age, Deucalion by the advice of Prometheus constructed a chest, and having stored it with provisions he embarked in it with Pyrrha. But Zeus by pouring heavy rain from heaven flooded the greater part of Greece, so that all men were destroyed, except a few who fled to the high mountains in the neighborhood. It was then that the mountains in Thessaly parted, and that all the world out-

side the Isthmus and Peloponnese was overwhelmed. But Deucalion, floating in the chest over the sea for nine days and as many nights, drifted to Parnassus, and there, when the rain ceased, he landed and sacrificed to Zeus, the god of Escape. And Zeus sent Hermes to him and allowed him to choose what he would, and he chose to get men. And at the bidding of Zeus he took up stones and threw them over his head, and the stones which Deucalion threw became men, and the stones which Pyrrha threw became women." Apollodorus, "Library," 1.7, perseus.tufts.edu, http://www.perseus.tufts.edu/hopper/text?doc=Perseus:text:1999.01.0022:text=Library:book=1:chapter=7&highlight=pyrrha. The source cited is as follows. Apollodorus. Apollodorus, The Library, with an English Translation by Sir James George Frazer, F.B.A., F.R.S. in 2 Volumes. Cambridge, MA, Harvard University Press; London, William Heinemann Ltd. 1921. Includes Frazer's notes.

In *Tradition, Concept and Claim* the Catholic philosopher Joseph Pieper's broad definition of sacred tradition helps to explain the similarities between various ancient creation and flood stories. He writes: "And yet it would be an inappropriate narrowing of the true state of affairs to see 'sacred tradition' realized only in the realm of biblical and Christian doctrine It is narrow-minded to define tradition, taken as process as act, as nothing more than 'the ecclesiastical proclamation of belief, which began with the Apostles…and was continued by their successors with the same authority.' Such a limitation of the term is even theologically questionable. Can one dispute so simply the claim of the mythical tradition in the pre- and non-Christian realm to preserve through the ages knowledge

Pyrrha, according to Apollodorus, was the daughter of Pandora, the first woman. Zeus, in Hesiod's *Works and Days*, created Pandora to get even with Prometheus who had favored men over gods including stealing fire and giving it to men at a time when the only humans who existed were men of the Golden Age.[4] After creating the first

---

which equally comes down from a divine source-especially insofar as we are convinced that there existed, long before the 'Apostles,' something like an 'original revelation'? This last concept, which we have mentioned before, does not have an especially high standing in the current discussion, if indeed it is mentioned at all. It has been at home in Christian theology, however, since the earliest times and it will always recur to memory as something indispensable. The concept of 'original revelation; betokens that at the beginning of history an event took place of a divine speech directed especially to 'the' man, that is to *all* men, and that time has entered into the sacred tradition of all peoples-in their myths, that is-and is preserved and present there, more or less recognizably. Augustine, in his late work the *Retractiones*, formulated this thought-admittedly in a way that is all too easy to understand and has in fact often been misunderstood: 'The very thing which is now called the 'Christian religion' existed among the ancients. Indeed it has never been absent since the beginning of the human race, until Christ appeared in the flesh. That was when the true religion, which already existed, began to be called the 'Christian religion.'" Josef Pieper, *Tradition Concept and Claim,* trans. E. Christian Kopff (Wilmington: ISI Books, 2008), 50-51.

[4] Hamilton, *Mythology*, 88.

woman, Zeus named her Pandora meaning the All-endowed because the gods on Olympus each gave her a gift that would act like "a plague to men."[5] When Pandora took off the lid of her gift, multiple curses flew out that in time would plague men.

Unlike Greek mythology, Babylonian mythology has a much more developed and coherent explanation of why and how human beings were created. In Babylonian mythology, higher class gods pitied the hard-working lower-class gods. To reduce the work load of the lower-class gods, the higher-class gods killed one of the lower-class gods and mixing the dead body with clay created men. The first men, therefore, were created from a violent act and in order to be slaves of the gods. After thousands of years, these human slaves multiplied so much that the noise they made disturbed the gods. In response, the gods decided to kill them by sending out a huge flood. One God, Enki, warns the man Atrahasis to build a boat to survive the flood. Atrahasis does so, and humans are saved from annihilation.[6]

The Genesis explanation of man's creation[7] is essen-

---

[5] Hesiod, "Works and Days," WD 80, perseus.tufts.edu, http://www.perseus.tufts.edu/hopper/text?doc=Perseus%3Atext%3A1999.01.0132%3Acard%3D59.

[6] "The Story of Atrahasis," faculty.gvsu.edu, http://faculty.gvsu.edu/websterm/Atrahasi.htm.

[7] In reference to the *Catechism of the Catholic Church* and the Pontifical Biblical Commission, Scott Hahn explains the historical elements within the first three chapters of Genesis. He writes, "The *Catechism of the Catholic Church*

tially different from the above Greek and Babylonian mythological explanations. In the described pagan myths, human beings are created to serve the gods, in Babylonian mythology, or, as implied in Greek mythology, to worship the gods and be like toys of the gods, as is particularly the case for the Titan Prometheus. In Genesis, however, God created man because God loves, is good, and wants to

---

speaks of 'the history of the fall narrated in Genesis' (#388), and asserts that 'the account of the fall in Genesis 3 uses figurative language, but affirms a primeval event, a deed that took place at the beginning of the history of man,' which was 'committed by our first parents' (#390). For authoritative guidance on the much harder question of what narrative elements of Genesis 1–3 should be regarded as historical, one should consult the Biblical Commission's *responsum*, 'On the Historical Character of the First Three Chapters of Genesis' (June 30, 1909), which lists nine 'narrated facts' whose 'literal and historical meaning' should not be 'called in question': (1) the creation of all things… by God at the beginning of time; (2) the special creation of man; (3) the formation of the first woman from man; (4) the unity of the human race; (5) the original happiness of our first parents in a state of justice, integrity and immortality; (6) the divine command laid upon man to prove his obedience; (7) the transgression of that divine command at the instigation of the devil under the form of a serpent; (8) the fall of our first parents from their primitive state of innocence; (9) the promise of a future redeemer." Scott Hahn, *A Father Who Keeps His Promises: God's Covenant Love in Scripture* (Cincinnati: Servant Books: 1998), loc. 3847.

share his goodness. God shared his love and goodness by creating human beings in His image. (Genesis 1:27)

Another important distinguishing feature within Genesis is that woman was created not as a punishment and source of evil and curses for man, but rather to complement man since God after looking at what He had made God says, "It is not good that man should be alone; I will make him a helper fit for him." (Genesis 2:18 RSV) Pitre points out that this is the first time in Genesis that in looking at something he has created he says something is not good.[8] Unlike the pagan myth of Pandora, the first woman, therefore, clearly is created good and is intended by God to be a source of goodness and blessings for man.

Chosen by God Out of Love

The Old Testament presents God's goodness and love in a particular way and in a universal way. God's love is directed to one, or a few, in that he chooses individuals and chooses Israel. God's love is for all since he chooses one and a few for the sake of all. Some are chosen for the sake of all, as the Old Testament scholar Fr. Richard Clifford explains, "With Noah and Abraham God uses one to address the whole. The whole is addressed through the one. One is selected, Israel, so all can be saved."[9]

The salvific relationship between God and Israel, de-

---

[8] Brant Pitre, *Jesus the Bridegroom: The Divine Love Story in the Bible,* CD 7 of 20 (Catholic Productions).

[9] Richard J, Clifford, "How the Bible Enriches Our Priestly Ministry," 2013 Annual Clergy Convocation of the Diocese of Norwich.

scribed repeatedly in the Old Testament, is a marital relationship, where God is a faithful, constant lover despite Israel's infidelities. God's marital covenant is prefigured in God's creation of Eve from Adam's side:

> So the Lord God caused a deep sleep to fall upon the man, and he slept; then he took one of his ribs and closed up its place with flesh. And the rib that the Lord God had taken from the man he made into a woman and brought her to the man. Then the man said, "This at last is bone of my bones and flesh of my flesh; this one shall be called Woman, for out of Man[e] this one was taken." Therefore a man leaves his father and his mother and clings to his wife, and they become one flesh. And the man and his wife were both naked, and were not ashamed. (Genesis 2:21-25 NRSV)

God established his marital covenant with Israel at Mount Sinai. Moses sealed this covenant by taking blood, dashing the blood on the Israelites and saying, "See the blood of the covenant that the Lord has made with you in accordance with these words." (Exodus 24: 8 NRSV) Brant Pitre in commenting on this passage explains, "From a biblical perspective, a 'covenant' was a *sacred family bond* between persons, establishing between them a permanent and sacred relationship."[10]

The marital aspect of the bond is made explicit in prophetic literature. For example, in Jeremiah we read, "I remember the devotion of your youth, your love as a bride,

---

[10] Pitre, *Jesus the Bridegroom*, 10.

Ch. 8: God as Bridegroom and Israel as Bride 129

how you followed me in the wilderness, in a land not sown. Israel was holy to the Lord, the first fruits of his harvest. All who ate of it were held guilty; disaster came upon them, says the Lord." (Jeremiah 2: 2-3 NRSV) Similarly, Ezekiel states, "I passed by you again and looked on you; you were at the age for love. I spread the edge of my cloak over you, and covered your nakedness: I pledged myself to you and entered into a covenant with you, says the Lord God, and you became mine." (Ezekiel 16:8 NRSV)[11] Isaiah even identifies the very land of Israel as part of what God marries with, "You shall no more be termed Forsaken, and your land shall no more be termed Desolate; but you shall be called My Delight Is in Her, and your land Married; for the Lord delights in you, and your land shall be married." (Isaiah 62: 4 NRSV)

Extra biblical Jewish tradition even more explicitly depicts the relationship between God and Israel as a marriage. For example, Pitre points out, Rabbi Jose in the *Mekilta on Exodus* 19:17 writes, "'The Lord came from Sinai,' to receive Israel as a bridegroom comes forth to meet the bride."[12]

The reason God chose Israel was not because Israel merited God's love but rather because, as the *Catechism of the Catholic Church* explains, "his sheer gratuitous love."[13] In indicating God's unconditional love, Deuteronomy states, "Because he loved your ancestors he chose their descend-

---

[11] Ibid., 10-13.
[12] Ibid., 12-13.
[13] "Catechism of the Catholic Church," no. 218, http://www.vatican.va/archive/ccc_css/archive/catechism/p1s2c1p1.htm.

ants after them." (Deuteronomy 4:37 NRSV) "It was because the Lord loved you and kept the oath that he swore to your ancestors, that the Lord has brought you out with a mighty hand, and redeemed you from the house of slavery, from the hand of Pharaoh king of Egypt." (Deuteronomy 7:8 NRSV) "[T]he Lord set his heart in love on your ancestors alone and chose you, their descendants after them, out of all the peoples, as it is today." (Deuteronomy 10:15 NRSV)

God's love for Israel is "everlasting" (Isaiah 54:8 NRSV) even when Israel is unfaithful in love because God's love is formed by his truth and holiness. In affirming God's truth, Psalm 118:160 states, "The sum of your word is truth; and every one of your righteous ordinances endures forever." (NRSV)[14] Along with repeatedly describing God as true, the Old Testament also frequently asserts there is no holiness like God's holiness, "There is no Holy One like the Lord".[15] (1 Samuel 2:2 NRSV) God proclaimed his faithful love to Moses after Moses cut the second set of stone tablets with, "The Lord, the Lord, a God merciful and gracious, slow to anger, and abounding in

---

[14] Also see 2 Samuel 7:28 NRSV "And now, O Lord God, you are God, and your words are true, and you have promised this good thing to your servant"; Deuteronomy 7:9 NRSV "Know therefore that the Lord your God is God, the faithful God who maintains covenant loyalty with those who love him and keep his commandments, to a thousand generation".

[15] Also see Exodus 15:1; Leviticus 19:2 1 Samuel 2:2; Psalm 22:3; Psalm 77:13; Song of Songs; Isaiah 43:15 57:15.

steadfast love and faithfulness, keeping steadfast love for the thousandth generation, forgiving iniquity and transgression and sin, yet by no means clearing the guilty, but visiting the iniquity of the parents upon the children and the children's children, to the third and the fourth generation." (Exodus 34:6-7 NRSV)

Israel's Marital Obligations

As the above verse 7 from Exodus 34 indicates, although God will love Israel regardless what Israel does, He will not ignore violations of the marital covenant but will punish the violators. The reason is once again because God loves Israel and as a good lover wants His beloved to be happy. Since sin is misery, Israel needs to be punished so as to gain sufficient freedom to detach herself from sinful patterns that cause her to be miserable. For this reason, explains Hosea, God brought Israel out of Egypt into the desert. (Hosea 2:14-15)

After Israel had spent a time of purification in the desert, God established his marital covenant with Israel through Moses. During the union, God, "spoke to Moses saying: Speak to all the congregation of the people of Israel and say to them: You shall be holy, for I the Lord your God am holy. You shall each revere your mother and father, and you shall keep my sabbaths: I am the Lord." (Leviticus 19:2-3 NRSV) Because God is holy, because He is loving, faithful and true, Israel also is to be holy, loving, faithful and true. The ultimate reason for the moral aspects of the law given on Sinai, therefore, is not to maintain peace among people in a horizontal manner but is found vertically, because God is holy and Israel in her union with

God her spouse is likewise to be holy.

For this reason, when members of Israel broke the law, they punished the violator not primarily to deter other potential violators but rather, explains Anthony Phillips, so that "no divine action might be taken against them."[16] Similarly, the love and justice Israelites are to do is also primarily to be done because God is just and is loving. Deuteronomy indicates this with, "For the Lord your God is God of gods and Lord of lords, the great God, mighty and awesome, who is not partial and takes no bribe, who executes justice for the orphan and the widow, and who loves the strangers, providing them food and clothing. You shall also love the stranger." (Deuteronomy 10:17-19 NRSV)

Due to Israel's marriage with God, idolatry, the worship of false Gods, is described repeatedly in the Old Testament as adultery. For this reason, Isaiah calls Israel, represented by Daughter Zion and Jerusalem, a "whore" (Isaiah 1:21 NRSV), and Jeremiah calls her a "faithless wife." (Jeremiah 3:20 NRSV)

Chapter 8 Discussion Questions

1. Contrast the Greek and Babylonian myths on the creation of human beings with the Old Testament's explanation. Include the following in your response: Zeus, Prometheus, Pandora, murdered lower-class God, slaves, creation of Adam, Genesis 2:18, creation of Eve.

---

[16] Anthony Phillips, *Ancient Israel's Criminal Law* (New York: Schocken Books, 1970) 11.

Ch. 8: God as Bridegroom and Israel as Bride   133

2. Describe the marital relationship between God and Israel. Include the following in your response: relationship of the part to the whole, after Egypt and in the desert, marital covenant at Mount Sinai, unmerited love, unconditional love, punishment for sin.

3. According to the Old Testament, what are Israel's marital obligations to God and why? Include the following in your response: holiness, loving, faithfulness, idolatry, sin.

Chapter 9

Jesus as Bridegroom and the Church as Bride

Introduction

Jesus fulfills in the flesh the role of bridegroom that the Old Testament foreshadowed when describing God as the bridegroom and Israel as His bride. As Pitre states, "Jesus' actions are meant to signal that he is not only the Jewish Messiah; he is *the divine Bridegroom come in person, to fulfill the prophecies of a new marriage covenant.*"[1] John the Baptist, in Pitre's interpretation, is the first in Scripture to publicly identify Jesus as the Messianic bridegroom with, "'I am not the Messiah, but I have been sent ahead of him.' He who has the bride is the bridegroom. The friend of the bridegroom, who stands and hears him, rejoices greatly at the bridegroom's voice. For this reason my joy has been fulfilled. He must increase, but I must decrease."[2] (John 3:28-30 NRSV)

In this chapter, we will examine Jesus as bridegroom by focusing on the Wedding at Cana, Jesus' meeting with the Samaritan woman at the well, the Eucharist, the Paschal Mystery, and Jesus' Second Coming. The chapter will conclude with a reflection on Christian Marriage.

---

[1] Brant Pitre, *Jesus the Bridegroom: The Greatest Love Story Ever Told* (New York: Image, 2014), 29.
[2] Ibid., 53.

Wedding at Cana

At the Wedding of Cana, Jesus publicly revealed his identity as the divine bridegroom in person who was foreshadowed in the Old Testament. Mary also assisted in introducing Jesus to the world as the bridegroom of the New Israel. Adeline Fehribach explains in *The Women in the Life of the Bridegroom,* "When the mother of Jesus says to Jesus, 'They have no wine' (2:3), she places him in the role of the bridegroom, whose responsibility it is to provide the wine."[3] Jesus' action at the Wedding at Cana of providing a superabundance of wine, Fehribach argues, indicates that "he was no ordinary bridegroom."[4] He is no ordinary bridegroom because he is the messianic bridegroom of Israel foretold by the Old Testament.[5]

The Cana marriage banquet that Jesus was at was a sign of a future marriage banquet in which Jesus would be the bridegroom. Jesus', interprets Pitre, indicates that this marriage banquet is in the future with His words to Mary, "My hour has not yet come."[6] (John 2:4 NRSV) The hour of Jesus' marriage banquet began at the Last Supper. There, instead of turning water into wine, he gave his blood under the appearance of wine while saying "this is

---

[3] Adeline Fehribach, *The Women in the Life of the Bridegroom* (Collegeville: The Liturgical Press, 1998), 29; cf. Pitre, *Jesus the Bridegroom*, 45.

[4] Fehribach, *The Women in the Life of the Bridegroom,* 29; cf. Pitre, *Jesus the Bridegroom*, 45.

[5] Fehribach, *The Women in the Life of the Bridegroom,* 30; cf. Pitre, *Jesus the Bridegroom*, 45.

[6] Pitre, *Jesus the Bridegroom*, 46.

my blood of the covenant".[7] (Matthew 26:28 NRSV)

Samaritan Woman

Another way Jesus revealed He is the messianic bridegroom was by sitting with and talking to a Samaritan woman at a well. To understand the significance of these actions, it is necessary to know the Old Testament's background regarding wells. In the Old Testament, wells were common locations where men met their future wives since women were tasked with drawing water. For example, demonstrates Pitre, Abraham's servant goes to a well to find a suitable, generous woman to be the wife for Isaac. By offering the servant and his camels water, Rebekkah demonstrated to the servant that she was a suitable wife for Isaac. (Genesis 24:1-67)[8]

Isaac's son Jacob similarly found a wife, Rachel, at a well (Genesis 29:1-14 NRSV), and Moses met his future wife Zipporah at a well (Exodus 2:15-22). In all three examples, a foreigner (Abraham, Isaac, and Moses) obtain a wife who is first met at a well. In light of this biblical, and also historical background of wells being common places to meet a potential wife, Fehribach comments that the disciples were surprised with Jesus talking with the Samaritan woman at a well not because she was a woman, because they did not express amazement before when Jesus related to women, but rather because of the combination of factors including Jesus as a foreigner in Samaria, and he is

---

[7] Pitre, *Jesus the Bridegroom*, 54.

[8] Brant Pitre, *JesusBrideGroomOutline,* CD and Outline (Catholic Productions), 54, CD 11.

talking with a woman at a well.⁹

Through the Samaritan woman as a representative of the Samaritan's corporate sin of intermingling the Israelite religion with idol worship, Jesus offers himself to be their messianic bridegroom and not only the messianic bridegroom of the Jewish people. Since the Samaritans were ancestors of Israelites who had intermarried with Gentiles settled by the Assyrian conquerors of 722 B.C., Jesus through the Samaritan woman, offers himself to be the messianic bridegroom of all people. (2 Kings 17:21-23) Jesus indicates his Catholic (universal) messiahship by saying, "'If you knew the gift of God, and who it is that is saying to you, 'Give me a drink,' you would have asked him, and he would have given you living water.'" (John 4: 10 NRSV)[10]

The reference to living water has an important context that helps to interpret Jesus' words. Pitre explains that for ancient Jews "living water" at times referred to water of a ritual bath a Jewish woman would take before she married.[11] By promising to give living water, Jesus, therefore, is not only promising to give the living water that the prophet Ezekiel had a vision of, where life giving water flowed out of the side of the Temple (Ezekiel 47:1-12), but also,

---

⁹ Fehribach, *The Women in the Life of the Bridegroom*, 50-51; cf. Pitre, *JesusBrideGroomOutline,* CD and Outline (Catholic Productions), 59.

[10] Fehribach, *The Women in the Life of the Bridegroom*, 67; Pitre, *JesusBrideGroomOutline,* CD and Outline (Catholic Productions), 59; Pitre, *Jesus the Bridegroom*, 61.

[11] Pitre, *Jesus the Bridegroom*, 70. Pitre cites Song of Songs 4:12, 15; *Joseph and Aseneth* 14:12-17.

explains Pitre, Jesus is promising to give the temple in person as the messianic bridegroom. The life-giving water that flows out of the Temple prophesied by Ezekiel is fulfilled by the water and blood which flowed from the pierced side of Jesus as he hung on the cross. The water represents Baptism, and the blood represents the Eucharist. (CCC no. 1225) Through Baptism, Jesus cleanses his bride not physically but spiritually, by washing away sin. In this way, Baptism prepares a Christian to receive the Eucharist, the wedding banquet of the bridegroom.[12]

The *Catechism of the Catholic Church* on Baptism and Eucharist explains,

> The entire Christian Life bears the mark of the spousal love of Christ and the Church. Already Baptism, the entry into the People of God, is a nuptial mystery; it is so to speak the nuptial bath which precedes the wedding feast, the Eucharist.[13]

Eucharist

Pitre describes the Last Supper as the wedding banquet of Jesus, anticipated at the Wedding of Cana because "[i]f Jesus is the Bridegroom and the Church is his bride, the Lord's Supper is not just a memorial, or a banquet of 'thanksgiving,' or a sacrifice; it is also a wedding banquet in

---

[12] Ibid., 73-78.
[13] "Catechism of the Catholic Church," no. 1617, http://ccc.usccb.org/flipbooks/catechism/files/assets/basic-html/page-422.html.

which Jesus gives himself entirely to his bride in a new and everlasting marriage covenant."[14] In other words, because Jesus fulfills the Old Testament and its types, in addition to being a memorial, a thanksgiving sacrificial meal, the Eucharist is also a wedding banquet. Those, therefore, who are invited to the "marriage supper of the Lamb" (Revelation 19:9 NRSV) are "to rejoice and exult."[15] (Revelation 19:7 NRSV)

Recall that Moses at Mount Sinai sealed God's marital covenant with Israel by throwing blood on the Israelites and saying, "See the blood of the covenant that the Lord has made with you in accordance with these words." (Exodus 24: 8 NRSV) Similarly, as the fulfillment of Moses the lawgiver by being law in person, Jesus seals the New Covenant with his own blood by giving his blood to his disciples. Scott Hahn relates blood to the sealing of all marital covenants:

> When two become one in marriage, the bridegroom gives the bride his flesh and blood; the bride receives him, his flesh and blood. (The Greek word *haima*, usually translated "blood," can refer to other bodily fluids, including the man's "seed." See Jn 1:13.) When he gives and she receives, they bring new life into the world. When does Christ, the Bridegroom, unite himself with his Bride? When does he give his flesh and blood in order to bring new life? In the Eucharist. The Eucharist is the sacrament of the consummation of the marriage between Christ and his Church. In the

---

[14] Pitre, *Jesus the Bridegroom*, 145.
[15] Ibid., 145.

Eucharist he renews the New Covenant, which is his marriage covenant with her. It is much more than a banquet. It is a wedding feast. We the Bride receive our Bridegroom's Body in the Eucharist. The marital imagery of Christ's love for his Church becomes a powerful symbol for the sacrament of marriage. Or is marriage a powerful symbol of Christ's love for his Church—for each of us?[16]

The sealing of the New Testament marital covenant followed by a heavenly marital banquet was, Pitre points out, prophesied by the prophets.[17]

The days are surely coming, says the Lord, when I will make a new covenant with the house of Israel and the house of Judah. It will not be like the covenant that I made with their ancestors when I took them by the hand to bring them out of the land of Egypt—a covenant that they broke, though I was their husband, says the Lord. But this is the covenant that I will make with the house of Israel after those days, says the Lord: I will put my law within them, and I will write it on their hearts; and I will be their God, and they shall be my people. No longer shall they teach one another, or say to each other, "Know the Lord," for they shall all know me, from the least of them to the greatest, says the Lord; for I will forgive their iniquity, and remem-

---

[16] Scott Hahn, *A Father Who Keeps His Promises: God's Covenant Love in Scripture* (Cincinnati: St. Anthony Messenger Press, 1998), 255.

[17] Pitre, *Jesus the Bridegroom*, 50.

ber their sin no more. (Jeremiah 31:31-34 NRSV)

On this mountain the Lord of hosts will make for all peoples a feast of rich food, a feast of well-aged wines, of rich food filled with marrow, of well-aged wines strained clear. And he will destroy on this mountain the shroud that is cast over all peoples, the sheet that is spread over all nations; he will swallow up death forever. Then the Lord God will wipe away the tears from all faces, and the disgrace of his people he will take away from all the earth, for the Lord has spoken. It will be said on that day, Lo, this is our God; we have waited for him, so that he might save us. This is the Lord for whom we have waited; let us be glad and rejoice in his salvation. (Isaiah 25:6-9 NRSV)

The Passion, Crucifixion, Resurrection and Second Coming

In the Gospel of Mark, Jesus proclaims himself a messianic bridegroom while indirectly referring to his future crucifixion when his marriage with his bride will be consummated. "The wedding guests cannot fast while the bridegroom is with them, can they? As long as they have the bridegroom with them, they cannot fast. The days will come when the bridegroom is taken away from them, and then they will fast on that day." (Mark 2:19-20 NRSV) The ancient Jews had a custom to mourn when the bridegroom, after celebrating for one week with the people, left to be alone with his bride. Similarly, Jesus' death on the cross is the moment when He leaves to be alone with his bride.[18]

In addition to identifying Jesus' wedding day as "the day of his death, the day of his crucifixion," Pitre also insightfully interprets details from Christ's Passion and Crucifixion as symbolic signs that Christ is consummating his marriage with his bride, the Church. (John 19:30 DRA "It is consummated")

Christ's crown of thorns may be taken as signaling that He is a bridegroom, explains Pitre, because in ancient Jewish tradition, bridegrooms wore crowns. For example, the Song of Songs states, "Look on King Solomon wearing a crown, the crown with which his mother crowned him on

---

[18] Pitre, *Jesus the Bridegroom*, 86-91, 116-118. Pitre cites Genesis 29:26-27. Pitre quotes Adeline Fehribach, [T]he wedding ceremony of the first century was essentially the groom's induction of the bride into his house…. Thus, Jesus' words could have been viewed within the context of the messianic bridegroom taking his bride into his Father's house." Brant Pitre, *Jesus the Bridegroom: The Greatest Love Story Ever Told* (New York: Image, 2014), 118; Scott Hahn describes the sign of the cross, which reminds Catholics of Jesus' sacrificial love, as "a summary of the faith in one single gesture." This is because the Jesus redemptive death, the trinity, and that God is family because he is triune all are implied by this simple gesture. That God is Father, Son and Holy Spirit, strongly emphasizes Hahn, is not an academic way by which God is tamed and domesticated but rather is a revelation of who God is in his very nature that "God is love." (1 John 4:8 NRSV) Scott Hahn, *How to Make Sense Out of the Mass*, CD (St. Joseph Communications, 2005).

the day of his wedding, the day his heart rejoiced." (Song of Songs 3:11 NRSV)[19]

The seamless tunic for which the Roman soldiers played lots after crucifying Jesus (John 19:23), argues Pitre, represents both priestly garments, since Jesus is the one, true, High Priest, and represents Jesus, the Bridegroom, since traditionally bridegrooms wore the garments of a priest.[20] The seamless garment represents Jesus' priestly nature since, according to Exodus and Leviticus, a priestly garment is to be made so that it "may not be torn."[21] (Exodus 28:32 NRSV cf. Leviticus 21:10)

According to Pitre, as mentioned previously, the water that flowed from Jesus' side after being pierced with a spear (John 19:34) is the fulfillment of the cleansing water in which a Jewish woman ritually bathes herself before her wedding and the water that flowed from the side of the Temple in Ezekiel's vision (Ezekiel 47:1-12).[22] The water that flowed from Jesus' side, representing Baptism, prepares for the wedding banquet of the Eucharist, represented by the blood that flowed from Jesus' pierced side.

Finally, Pitre presents Jesus' paschal mystery as "a recapitulation of Adam and Eve"[23] where the New Adam is Christ and the New Eve is the Church. To support his recapitulation explanation, Pitre refers to St. Paul' Letter to the Ephesians where Paul commands husbands to love

---

[19] Pitre, *Jesus the Bridegroom*, 103. Pitre cites *The Song of Solomon* 3:11.

[20] Ibid., 106.

[21] Ibid. Pitre cites Josephus, *Antiquities* 3:161.

[22] Ibid., 76.

[23] Ibid., 112.

their wives as Christ loved his Church by dying and giving "himself up for her, in order to make her holy by cleansing her." (Ephesians 5:25-26 NRSV) "Thus," writes Pitre, "the day of Jesus' crucifixion is his wedding day, when he, the new Adam is 'joined (Greek *proskollao*) to his wife,' the Church, in an everlasting covenant."[24]

However, only when Jesus comes in his resurrected state at the end of time will he and his bride the Church be definitively united. Pitre writes, "[J]ust as the Jewish Bible *begins* with the marriage of Adam and Eve, the New Testament *ends* with the marriage of God and humanity in the great 'wedding supper' at the end of time (Revelation 19:7)."[25]

Christian Marriage

In interpreting Paul's comparison of Christ's death on the cross to marriage, Pitre clarifies:

Paul is *not* saying that the relationship between Christ and the Church is 'like' a human marriage. That would be getting him completely backwards. To the contrary, Paul is saying that Christian marriage between a man and a woman should be *like* the supernatural love be-

---

[24] Ibid., 112. In contrast with the Judeo-Christian understanding of marriage, C.S. Lewis, in "We have no 'Right to Happiness'" presents the Western understanding of sex, even in marriage, as just "four bare legs in a bed." C.S. Lewis, *God in the Dock: Essays on Theology and Ethics* (Grand Rapids: Eerdmans Publishing Company, 1970), 357.

[25] Pitre, *Jesus the Bridegroom*, 115.

tween Christ and the Church. It is Christ's relationship with the Church that is the 'great mystery' (Greek *mysterion mega*) to which Christian marriage must look as its model (Ephesians 5:32).[26]

When Christ's relationship with the Church is understood as the ultimate marriage in its full truth upon which all others are to be patterned while always falling short, the meaning of Catholic marriages becomes more evident. Unlike a purely civil marriage, which is essentially a contract, and unlike the Old Testament marriages which form a sacred family bond by a covenant, a Christian marriage, explains Pitre, is to be "a *living icon* of the sacrificial spousal love between Christ and the Church."[27] This means that not only is a Catholic couple to bond with one another and be open to life with the hope for babies, but they are also to be mutually concerned with the other's sanctification because what they are participating in is a sacred sacrament. As a sacrament, marriage is a sacred sign of the invisible reality of God's eternal love, specifically Jesus' love for his bride the Church.[28]

Since Jesus demonstrated his love for his bride the Church sacrificially by laying down his life for her, in a Christian marriage that is to be a participation in Christ's love for his Church, men are not to lead by, writes Pitre, "domination or intimidation."[29] This is clear in how Paul instructs Christians to relate to one another within mar-

---

[26] Ibid., 153.
[27] Ibid., 151.
[28] Ibid., 153, 158.
[29] Ibid., 156.

riage and distinguishes a Christian understanding on marriage from the Greek and Roman understanding. Charles J. Reid explains:

> Christianity, in its earliest forms, adopted and adapted some aspects of the Greco-Roman synthesis on marriage and rejected other aspects altogether. It has been observed that many early Christian metaphors tended to be subversive of the language of authority that surrounded the Roman legal conception of the family. Where Roman law emphasized hierarchical power and submission, Christian metaphors focused on equality. In a frequently analyzed passage, after all, St. Paul boldly proclaimed that "There is neither Jew nor Greek, there is neither slave nor freeman, there is neither male or female. For you are all one in Christ Jesus.[30]

This Christian transformation of Roman and Greek terminology and structures by emphasizing equality more by considering God as Our Father, does not mean, though, that St. Paul in Ephesians is teaching that the husband is to lack leadership in his family in a way where wives and husbands are to be mutually subordinate to one another without distinction. Paul clearly states, rather, that "the husband is head of his wife just as Christ is head of his body the church". (Ephesians 5:23 NAB) In this verse

---

[30] Charles J. Reid Jr., *Power of the Body, Equality in the Family: Rights and Domestic Relations in Medieval Canon Law* (Grand Rapids: William B. Eerdmans Publishing Company, 2004), 72.

the leadership of the husband is described with the metaphor of head, (traditionally representing objectivity, logic and law) while implying the wife's leadership with the heart (traditionally representing subjectivity, the personal, prudence, and wisdom).[31] As Pitre comments, "A headless person is a dead person and a heartless is a dead person. The question is the head or heart more important is meaningless since they both need each other in an essential way. The man is naturally ordered to governing, and the woman is naturally ordered to loving. The end is peace and harmony at home."[32]

Virgins and celibates, in other words religious sisters and celibate priests, also are sacred signs of the invisible reality of Jesus' spousal, sacrificial love but in a different, complementary manner. Married couples are signs pointing to what is to come. Virgins and celibates are signs of a reality that has already come but in a not yet perfected state. In heaven, we all will be married to God, and for this reason physical marriages between individuals will cease since they will lose their meaning.[33]

---

[31] Scott Hahn, *First Comes Love: Finding Your Family in the Church and the Trinity* (New York: Doubleday, 2002), 171-172. "Traditionally we identify fatherhood, the masculine principle, with law, logic, and objectivity. Motherhood we associate with love, wisdom, and profound subjective insight."

[32] Pitre, *JesusBrideGroomOutline*, CD 15.

[33] Pitre, *Jesus the Bridegroom*, 153, 158. Pitre references John Paul II's *Pastores Dabo Vobis*, no. 22.

Chapter 9 Discussion Questions

1. Discuss how Jesus the divine bridegroom is foreshadowed in the Wedding at Cana. Include the following in your response: at least two relevant Old Testament references, messianic bridegroom, symbolism of the Wedding at Cana.

2. Discuss how Jesus the divine bridegroom is foreshadowed by His sitting with a Samaritan woman at a well. Include the following in your response: at least two relevant Old Testament references, wells, Samaritan religious practices, living water.

3. Discuss how Jesus the divine bridegroom is foreshadowed by His instituting the Eucharist. Include the following in your response: at least two relevant Old Testament references, wedding banquet, blood.

4. Discuss how Jesus the divine bridegroom is foreshadowed by the Paschal Mystery, and by His Second Coming. Include the following in your response: At least two relevant references from Scripture, crown of thorns, seamless tunic, water and blood, recapitulation, Second Coming.

5. Discuss the meaning of Catholic Marriage in light of Jesus the divine bridegroom. Include the following in your response: Ephesians, contract, covenant, sacrament of marriage, virgins and celibates.

Chapter 10

Early Church and the Magisterium on Marriage

Introduction

Aided by the Holy Spirit, the early Church Fathers further developed the understanding of Jesus as Bridegroom and the Church as bride in multiple ways. We will look at a few of these before moving on to magisterial teachings on marriage.

Early Church on Marriage

St. Leo the Great's positive concept of our Christian identity helps to properly situate the early Church's understanding of marriage. In accordance with Scripture's teaching that we are "participants of the divine nature" (2 Peter 1:4 NRSV), St. Leo the Great (c. 400-461) exhorted:

> Christian, remember your dignity, and now that you share in God's own nature, do not return by sin to your former base condition. Bear in mind who is your head and of whose body you are a member. Do not forget that you have been rescued from the power of darkness and brought into the light of God's king-

dom.[1]

St. John Chrysostom (c. 349-407) in his commentary on Ephesians chapter five locates the dignity of a Christian marriage within the context of Christ's mystical body, specifically His love for His bride the Church. In commenting on verse 26, Chrysostom reminds husbands that in marrying the Church, Christ loved her even though her members were deformed and dirtied by sin. Furthermore, despite faults of her members, Christ is so faithful to his bride that He even died on the cross for her. After the example of Christ, Christian husbands are to be faithful to their wives:

> He gave himself up for her that "He might cleanse and sanctify her..." (v. 26). So the Church was not pure. She had blemishes, she was ugly and cheap. Whatever kind of wife you marry, you will never take a bride like Christ did when he married the Church; you will never marry anyone estranged from you as the Church was from Christ. Despite all this, he did not abhor or hate

---

[1] Leo the Great, "Christian Remember Your Dignity-St. Leo," https://www.crossroadsinitiative.com/media/articles/christian-remember-your-dignity-st-leo/. The following source was cited: Sermo 1 in Nativitate Domini, 1-3; PL 54, 190-193. This sermon appears in the Liturgy of the Hours as the second reading on Christmas Day. http://www.crossroadsinitiative.com/library_article/359/Christian_Remember_Your_Dignity__St._Leo.html

her for her extraordinary corruption.[2]

Later in his commentary, Chrysostom encourages men not to place undue importance on "outward beauty" since such beauty is often:

> full of conceit and licentiousness; it makes men jealous, and fills men with lustful thought. But does it give any pleasure? Perhaps for one or two months, or a year at most but then no longer; ... The love that began on honest grounds still continues ardently, since its object is beauty of the soul and not of the body. ... Look for affection, gentleness, and humility in a wife; these are tokens of beauty.[3]

---

[2] St. John Chrysostom, *On Marriage and Family Life*, trans. Catherine P. Roth & David Anderson (New York: St. Vladimir's Seminary Press, 2003), 47; Brant Pitre, *JesusBrideGroomOutline,* CD and Outline (Catholic Productions), 74; The International Theological Commission clarifies the relationship of sin to the Catholic Church by explaining that the Catholic Church is not "a subject who sins" but rather one who "assum[es] the weight of her children's faults in maternal solidarity." International Theological Commission, *Memory and Reconciliation: The Church and the Faults of the Past December 1999*, 3.4, The Vatican, http://www.vatican.va/roman_curia/congregations/cfaith/cti_documents/rc_con_cfaith_doc_20000307_memory-reconc-itc_en.html.

[3] St. John Chrysostom, *On Marriage and Family Life*, 48-49; Pitre, *JesusBrideGroomOutline,* 76.

In teaching that marriage does not only consist of babies and bonding but also, due to its sacramental nature, is a sanctifying reality he writes:

> Tell her that you love her more than your own life, because this present life is nothing, and that your only hope is that the two of you pass through this life in such a way that in the world to come you will be united in perfect love. Say to her, "Our time here is brief and fleeting, but if we are pleasing to God, we can exchange this life for the Kingdom to come. Then we will be perfectly one both with Christ and each other, and our pleasure will know no bounds.[4]

In the above passage, Pitre points out, Chrysostom does not teach that in heaven earthly marriages will be terminated but rather teaches that in heaven earthly marriages will be fulfilled and heightened to their utmost potential. The reason, Pitre explains, is that in heaven "spouses will be infinitely closer when the earthly sign of marriage gives way to the eternal reality of perfect union with God and one another."[5]

Along with affirming the great dignity of Christian marriage, Chrysostom, in commenting on Paul, provides practical advice for a well-ordered household. Such a household is not a relationship "where there is equal authority.... A household cannot be a democracy, ruled by everyone, but the authority must necessarily rest in one

---

[4] St. John Chrysostom, *On Marriage and Family Life*, 61; Pitre, *Jesus the Bridegroom*, 156.

[5] Pitre, *Jesus the Bridegroom*, 156.

Ch. 10: Early Church and the Magisterium on Marriage   155

person."[6] Due to this natural requirement, Chrysostom writes, "Paul places the head in authority and the body in obedience for the sake of peace."[7] The ultimate reason Chrysostom provides once again is Christ's relationship to His Church. Chrysostom explains, "The same is true for the Church: when men are led by the Spirit of Christ then there is peace."[8] Chrysostom identifies the authority, the one who represents Christ the head with the father, and the heart of the body with the wife:

> St. Paul would not speak so earnestly about this subject without serious reason; why else would he say, "Wives, be subject to your husbands, as to the Lord?" Because when harmony prevails, the children are raised well, the household is kept in order, and neighbors, friends and relatives praise the result. Great benefits, both for families and states, are thus produced. When it is otherwise, however, everything is thrown into confusion and turned upside-down.[9]

In responding to the objection that respectful obedience to a husband (Ephesians 5:33) is in tension with the dynamics of love, Chrysostom responds:

> How, one may say, is there to be love where there is

---

[6] St. John Chrysostom, *On Marriage and Family Life*, 53; Pitre, *JesusBrideGroomOutline*, 73.

[7] Ibid.

[8] Ibid.

[9] St. John Chrysostom, *On Marriage and Family Life*, 44-45; Pitre, *JesusBrideGroomOutline*, 73.

respect? Love is most powerfully present when accompanied by respect. For what she loves she also reveres, and what she reveres she also loves. She reveres him as the head and loves him as a member of the whole body. God's purpose in ordering marriage is peace. One takes the husband's role, one takes the wife's role, one in guiding, one in supporting. If both have the very same roles, there would be no peace. The house is not rightly governed when all have precisely the same roles. There must be a differentiation of roles under a single head.[10]

The common vicious attitude of husbands who do assume the leadership role in their families to which Chrysostom calls attention is "threatening, lording it over her or intimidating her."[11] On the other hand, the common vicious attitude of wives to husband leaders is "rejecting, hating, spurning, and nagging him."[12]

Pitre comments on this aspect of Chrysostom's writing *On Marriage and Family* in two ways, first in relationship to a marriage between a husband and a wife, and second in relationship to the spiritual marriage between pastors and their flock. With respect to the first, Pitre writes,

---

[10] Thomas C. Oden, *Ancient Christian Commentary on Scripture, New Testament VIII Galatians, Ephesian, Philippians* (London: Routledge, 1999), 200; Pitre, *JesusBrideGroomOutline*, 71.

[11] Oden, *Ancient Christian Commentary on Scripture*, 185; Pitre, *Jesus the Bridegroom*, 155.

[12] Ibid., 185; Pitre, *Jesus the Bridegroom: The Greatest Love Story Ever Told* (New York: Image, 2014), 155.

"[B]ecause marriage is supposed to reflect Christ's love for the church, there is no excuse for male domination or intimidation. Likewise, when the Christian wife supports her husband and respects him by refusing to criticize him or tear him down, she too becomes a living icon of the Church's joyful response to the sacrificial love of Jesus the Bridegroom."[13] Similarly, priests are not to be abusive, and domineering towards those whom they lead, and those who are led, which includes priests in relationship to their bishops, are not to criticize and tear down their leaders.[14]

Along with understanding marriage from the perspective of Christ's marriage to the Church, the early Church also viewed baptism as a kind of marriage. For this reason, those to be baptized first disrobed, then were baptized and finally were clothed in white garments signifying the garments of a bride whose spouse is Christ.[15] A function of the early women helpers (*diakonissai*) was to assist women who disrobe and are baptized.[16]

---

[13] Pitre, *Jesus the Bridegroom*, 156.

[14] Pitre, *JesusBrideGroomOutline*, CD 15.

[15] Pitre, *Jesus the Bridegroom*, 142.

[16] The following early Christian document was written in the early 3rd century, and represents the teaching of the 12 Apostles. *Didascalia Apostolorum*, trans. R. Hugh Connolly (Oxford: Clarendon Press, 1929), http://earlychristianwritings.com/text/didascalia.html. Chapter XVI, On the Appointment of Deacons and Deaconesses, "[iii. 12] Wherefore, O bishop, appoint thee workers of righteousness as helpers who may co-operate with thee unto salvation. Those that please thee out of all the people thou shalt choose and appoint as deacons:? a man for the per-

formance of the most things that are required, but a woman for the ministry of women. For there are houses whither thou canst not send a deacon to the women, on account of the heathen, but mayest send a deaconess. Also, because in many other matters the office of a woman deacon is required. In the first place, when women go down into the water, those who go down into the water ought to be anointed by a deaconess with the oil of anointing; and where there is no woman at hand, and especially no deaconess, he who baptizes must of necessity anoint her who is being baptized. But where there is a woman, and especially a deaconess, it is not fitting that women should be seen by men:? but with the imposition of hand do thou anoint the head only. As of old the priests and kings were anointed in Israel, do thou in like manner, with the imposition of hand, anoint the head of those who receive baptism, whether of men or of women; and afterwards -- whether thou thyself baptize, or thou command the deacons or presbyters to baptize -- let a woman deacon, as we have already said, anoint the women. But let a man pronounce over them the invocation of the divine Names in the water.? And when she who is being baptized has come up from the water, let the deaconess receive her, and teach and instruct her how the seal of baptism ought to be (kept) unbroken in purity and holiness. For this cause we say that the ministry of a woman deacon is especially needful and important. For our Lord and Saviour also was ministered unto by women ministers, *Mary Magdalene, and Mary the daughter of James and mother of Jose, and the mother of the sons of Zebedee* [Mt 27.56], with other women beside. And thou also hast need of the ministry of a deaconess for many

Magisterial Teaching on Marriage

Although writing over 1,500 years after Chrysostom, Pope Pius XI in his Encyclical Letter on Christian Marriage (*Casti Connubii*) similarly affirmed the husband's role as the head of the family with the wife's role as the heart:

> This subjection, however, does not deny or take away the liberty which fully belongs to the woman both in view of her dignity as a human person, and in view of her most noble office as wife and mother and companion; nor does it bid her obey her husband's every request if not in harmony with right reason or with the dignity due to wife; nor, in fine, does it imply that the wife should be put on a level with those persons who in law are called minors, to whom it is not customary to allow free exercise of their rights on account of their lack of mature judgment, or of their ignorance of human affairs. But it forbids that exaggerated liberty which cares not for the good of the family; it forbids that in this body which is the family, the heart be separated from the head to the great detriment of the whole body and the proximate danger of ruin. For if the man is the head, the woman is the heart, and as he occupies the chief place in ruling, so she may and

---

things; for a deaconess is required to go into the houses of the heathen where there are believing women, and to visit those who are sick, and to minister to them in that of which they have need, and to bathe those who have begun to recover from sickness."

ought to claim for herself the chief place in love.[17]

Another example of similarities of thought between an early Church Father and a modern pope is between St. Augustine's bride and bridegroom analogies and John Paul II's. Both developed Revelation's marital imagery. Two examples from Augustine are below:

> "[In] those two original humans...the marriage of Christ and the Church was prefigured...[A]s Adam was a type of Christ, so too was the creation of Eve from the sleeping Adam a prefiguration of the creation of the Church from the side of the Lord as he slept, for as he suffered and died on the cross and was struck by a lance, the sacraments which formed the Church flowed forth from him. By Christ's sleeping we are also to understand his passion... As Eve came from the side of the sleeping Adam, so the Church was born from the side of the suffering Christ.[18]

> Like a bridegroom Christ went forth from his nuptial chamber ... He came even to the marriage-bed of the cross, and there, ascending it, he consummated a marriage. And when he sensed the creature sighing in her breath, he surrendered himself to torment for his bride

---

[17] Pius XI, "On Christian Marriage: *Casti Connubii*, December 21, 1930," no. 27, http://papalencyclicals.net/Pius11/P11CASTI.HTM.

[18] Pitre, *Jesus the Bridegroom*, 110. Pitre cites Augustine, *Exposition of the Psalms* 138:2.

in a communication of love.[19]

A particularly notable example of John Paul II's development of Revelation's marital imagery is from his apostolic letter on women, *Mulieris Dignitatem*. Here we read:

> 25. In the Letter to the Ephesians we encounter a second dimension of the analogy which, taken as a whole, serves to reveal the "great mystery". This is a symbolic dimension. If God's love for the human person, for the Chosen People of Israel, is presented by the Prophets as the love of the bridegroom for the bride, such an analogy expresses the "spousal" quality and the divine and non-human character of God's love: "For your Maker is your husband ... the God of the whole earth he is called" (Is 54:5). The same can also be said of the spousal love of Christ the Redeemer: "For God so loved the world that he gave his only Son" (Jn 3:16). It is a matter, therefore, of God's love expressed by means of the Redemption accomplished by Christ. According to Saint Paul's Letter, this love is "like" the spousal love of human spouses, but naturally it is not "the same". For the analogy implies a likeness, while at the same time leaving ample room for non-likeness.
>
> This is easily seen in regard to the person of the "bride". According to the Letter to the Ephesians, the bride is the Church, just as for the Prophets the bride

---

[19] Pitre, *Jesus the Bridegroom*, 92. Pitre cites Augustine, *Sermo Suppositus*, 120:3.

was Israel. She is therefore a collective subject and not an individual person. This collective subject is the People of God, a community made up of many persons, both women and men. "Christ has loved the Church" precisely as a community, as the People of God. At the same time, in this Church, which in the same passage is also called his "body" (cf. Eph 5:23), he has loved every individual person. For Christ has redeemed all without exception, every man and woman. It is precisely this love of God which is expressed in the Redemption; the spousal character of this love reaches completion in the history of humanity and of the world.

Christ has entered this history and remains in it as the Bridegroom who "has given himself". "To give" means "to become a sincere gift" in the most complete and radical way: "Greater love has no man than this" (Jn 15:13). According to this conception, all human beings - both women and men - are called through the Church, to be the "Bride" of Christ, the Redeemer of the world. In this way "being the bride", and thus the "feminine" element, becomes a symbol of all that is "human", according to the words of Paul: "There is neither male nor female; for you are all one in Christ Jesus" (Gal 3:28).

From a linguistic viewpoint we can say that the analogy of spousal love found in the Letter to the Ephesians links what is "masculine" to what is "feminine", since, as members of the Church, men too are included in the concept of "Bride". This should not surprise us, for Saint Paul, in order to express his mission in Christ and in the Church, speaks of the "little children with whom he is again in travail" (cf. Gal 4:19). In the sphere of what is "human" - of what is humanly personal - "masculinity" and "femininity" are distinct, yet at the same time they complete and explain each other. This is also present in the great analogy of the "Bride" in the Letter to the Ephesians. In the Church every human being - male and female - is the "Bride", in that he or she accepts the gift of the love of Christ the Redeemer, and seeks to respond to it with the gift of his or her own person.

Christ is the Bridegroom. This expresses the truth about the love of God who "first loved us" (cf. 1 Jn 4:19) and who, with the gift generated by this spousal love for man, has exceeded all human expectations: "He loved them to the end" (Jn 13:1). The Bridegroom - the Son consubstantial with the Father as God - became the son of Mary; he became the "son of man", true man, a male. The symbol of the Bridegroom is masculine. This masculine symbol represents the human aspect of the divine love which God has for Israel, for the Church, and for all people. Meditating on what the Gospels say about Christ's attitude towards women, we can conclude that as a man, a son of Israel, he revealed the dignity of the "daughters of Abraham" (cf. Lk 13:16), the dignity belonging to women from the very "beginning" on an equal footing with men. At the same time Christ emphasized the originality which distinguishes women from men, all the richness lavished upon women in the mystery of creation. Christ's attitude towards women serves as a model of what the Letter to the Ephesians expresses with the concept of "bridegroom". Precisely because Christ's divine love is the love of a Bridegroom, it is the model and pattern of all human love, men's love in particular.[20]

Benedict XVI further developed John Paul's II theology of marriage by writing specifically on love, especially on *eros* (desirous, wanting to receive love), and *agape* (giving love). In doing so, he inter-relates them and argues that in Christianity both types of loves are important. The receptive love of *eros* is proper to creatures since only God is the ultimate giver by being the Creator. Nonetheless, human *eros* needs to be transformed by agape love since we are called to participate in God's nature as giver:

> The more the two, in their different aspects, find a proper unity in the one reality of love, the more the true nature of love in general is realized. Even if *eros* is at first mainly covetous and ascending, a fascination for the great promise of happiness, in drawing near to the other, it is less and less concerned with itself, increasingly seeks the happiness of the other, is concerned more and more with the beloved, bestows itself and wants to "be there for" the other. The element of *agape* thus enters into this love, for otherwise *eros* is

---

[20] John Paul II, "Apostolic Letter, Mulieris Dignitatem," August 15, 1988, no. 25, http://w2.vatican.va/content/john-paul-ii/en/apost_letters/1988/documents/hf_jp-ii_apl_19880815_mulieris-dignitatem.html.

impoverished and even loses its own nature. On the other hand, man cannot live by oblative, descending love alone. He cannot always give, he must also receive. Anyone who wishes to give love must also receive love as a gift. Certainly, as the Lord tells us, one can become a source from which rivers of living water flow (cf. Jn 7:37-38). Yet to become such a source, one must constantly drink anew from the original source, which is Jesus Christ, from whose pierced heart flows the love of God (cf. Jn 19:34).

In the account of Jacob's ladder, the Fathers of the Church saw this inseparable connection between ascending and descending love, between *eros* which seeks God and *agape* which passes on the gift received, symbolized in various ways. In that biblical passage we read how the Patriarch Jacob saw in a dream, above the stone which was his pillow, a ladder reaching up to heaven, on which the angels of God were ascending and descending (cf. Gen 28:12; Jn 1:51). A particularly striking interpretation of this vision is presented by Pope Gregory the Great in his *Pastoral Rule*. He tells us that the good pastor must be rooted in contemplation. Only in this way will he be able to take upon himself the needs of others and make them his own: *"per pietatis viscera in se infirmitatem caeterorum transferat"*. Saint Gregory speaks in this context of Saint Paul, who was borne aloft to the most exalted mysteries of God, and hence, having descended once more, he was able to become all things to all men (cf. 2 Cor 12:2-4; 1 Cor 9:22). He also points to the example of Moses, who entered the tabernacle time and again, remaining in dialogue with God, so that when he emerged he could be at the service of his people. "Within [the tent] he is borne aloft through contemplation, while without he is completely engaged in helping those who suffer: *intus in contemplationem rapitur, foris infirmantium negotiis urgetur.*"[21]

We now turn our attention to spiritual marriage in which *eros* is called to be transformed in a particularly intensive manner by *agape* love. This spiritual marriage is expressed by two groups of people: virgins and celibates. While the married state was viewed in the early Church as a highly dignified state because of its relationship to Christ's love for the Church, virginity and celibacy were not seen as a lesser good but rather an even greater good. This belief is contained in Paul's first letter to the Corinthians where he writes:

> If anyone thinks that he is not behaving properly toward his fiancée, if his passions are strong, and so it has to be, let him marry as he wishes; it is no sin. Let them marry. But if someone stands firm in his resolve, being under no necessity but having his own desire under control, and has determined in his own mind to keep her as his fiancée, he will do well. So then, he who marries his fiancée does well; and he who refrains from marriage will do better. (1 Corinthians 7:36-38

---

[21] Benedict XVI, "Deus Caritas Est," December 25, 2005, no. 7, http://w2.vatican.va/content/benedict-xvi/en/encyclicals/documents/hf_ben-xvi_enc_20051225_deus-caritas-est.html.

NRSV)

Due to a loss of appreciation for the vocation to virginity and celibacy, the Council of Trent (1545-1563) decreed, "If any one saith, that the marriage state is to be placed above the state of virginity, or of celibacy, and that it is not better and more blessed to remain in virginity, or in celibacy, than to be united in matrimony; let him be anathema."[22] As Revelation teaches, and repeated by Trent, the choice between marriage and virginity or celibacy is a choice between two goods with virginity and celibacy being the better good for those who are called. While virginity and celibacy both shine forth Christ's perfect universal love in his marriage to his heavenly bride that earthly marriages only foreshadow,[23] the two do so in different and complementary manner.

Virgins represent the Church as the bride of Christ and celibates represent Christ as bride-groom. Pitre directs our attention to the Church's liturgy, where this is made explicit. For example, in its teaching on the Liturgy of the Hours, the *Catechism of the Catholic Church* states, "[T]he Liturgy of the Hours 'is truly the voice of the Bride herself addressed to her Bridegroom. It is the very prayer which Christ himself together with his Body addresses to the Father.'"[24] In a similar vein of thought, the *Rite of Consecration*

---

[22] "The Council of Trent: Doctrine on the Sacrament of Matrimony, Doctrine and Canons," http://thecounciloftrent.com/ch24.htm.

[23] Pitre, *Jesus the Bridegroom,* 163.

[24] "Catechism of the Catholic Church," no. 1174, http://www.vatican.va/archive/ ENG0015/__P39.HTM.

to a Life of Virginity reads:

> The Church is the bride of Christ. This title of the Church was given by the fathers and doctors of the Church to those like you who speak to us of the world to come, where there is not marrying or giving in marriage. You are a sign of the great mystery of salvation, proclaimed at the beginning of human history and fulfilled in the marriage covenant between Christ and his Church.[25]

Chapter 10 Discussion Questions

1. Discuss why the early Church viewed marriage with high regard. Include the follow-ing in your response: at least one reference to Scripture, at least one reference to St. John Chrysostom's *On Marriage and Family Life*, marriage and heaven.

---

[25] Pitre, *JesusBrideGroomOutline*, 88. In commenting on the attractive quality of religious sisters, Pitre speculated why some seminarians he knows develop "nun crushes." Pitre reasons that in a certain sense this "crush" is reasonable from the perspective of faith, if the bride of Christ is not pursued, since a religious sister "represents a beauty greater than any beauty we can encounter in this world and any pleasures we can encounter in this world, the beauty and joy of being fully united to God for all eternity in the beatific vision." Pitre, *JesusBrideGroomOutline*, CD 17.

2. Comment on Chrysostom's and Pope Pius XI's teaching on a well-ordered household. Include the following in your response: Ephesians 5, equality, role of the husband, role of the wife, vices of husbands, vices of wives, application of their teaching to priests and laity, and to priests and bishops.

3. Comment on the following excerpt from John Paul II, "In the Church every human being - male and female - is the 'Bride', in that he or she accepts the gift of the love of Christ the Redeemer, and seeks to respond to it with the gift of his or her own person." Do so in reference to Benedict's XVI explanation of *eros* and *agape*.

4. Explain how virginity and celibacy complement one another. In doing so include the terms bride and bridegroom while defining what you mean by these terms.

Chapter 11

Priests as Bridegrooms

Introduction

John Paul II, in his Apostolic Exhortation *Pastores Dabo Vobis*, calls priests "spouses of the Church":

> The priest is called to be the living image of Jesus Christ, the spouse of the Church. Of course, he will always remain a member of the community as a believer alongside his other brothers and sisters who have been called by the Spirit, but in virtue of his configuration to Christ, the head and shepherd, the priest stands in this spousal relationship with regard to the community. "Inasmuch as he represents Christ, the head, shepherd and spouse of the Church, the priest is placed not only in the Church but also in the forefront of the Church." In his spiritual life, therefore, he is called to live out Christ's spousal love toward the Church, his bride. Therefore, the priest's life ought to radiate this spousal character, which demands that he be a witness to Christ's spousal love and thus be capable of loving people with a heart which is new, generous and pure - with genuine self - detachment, with full, constant and faithful dedication and at the same time with a kind of "divine jealousy" (cf. 2 Cor. 11:2) and even with a kind of maternal tenderness, capable of bearing "the pangs of birth" until "Christ be

formed" in the faithful (cf. Gal. 4:19).[1]

We will reflect on these words of John Paul II first from the perspective of the glory of the priesthood, then from the priesthood as a calling to service, which necessarily in this world entails a cross.

The Glory of the Priesthood

The 1994 *Congregation for the Clergy Directory on the Ministry and Life of Priests* locates the priesthood in Jesus Christ who through sacramental ordination unites the priest to himself in way that affects the very being, the very essence of a priest. This change is an "ontological" change:

> Through the sacramental ordination conferred by the imposition of hands and the consecratory prayers of the Bishop, "a specific ontological bond which unites the priest to Christ, High Priest and Good Shepherd" is established. Thus, the identity of the priest comes from the specific participation in the Priesthood of Christ, in which the one ordained becomes, in the Church and for the Church, a real, living and faithful image of Christ the Priest, "a sacramental representation of Christ, Head and Shepherd". Through consecration, the priest "receives a spiritual 'power' as a gift which is a participation in the authority with which Je-

---

[1] John Paul II, "Pastores Dabo Vobis," March 25, 1992, no. 22, http://w2.vatican.va/content/john-paul-ii/en/apost_exhortations/documents/hf_jp-ii_exh_25031992_pastores-dabo-vobis.html.

Ch. 11: Priests as Bridegrooms

sus Christ, through his Spirit, guides the Church".[2]

Because of the permanent, ontological change ordination causes, the priesthood is not only defined by specific actions only a priest can perform, including confecting the Eucharist and absolving from sins, but also indicates an identity that is not based on function. The ontological identity is the priesthood's unique relationship with Christ, where, by virtue of ordination, he participates in the headship of Christ as spouse of the Church, as bridegroom, and as shepherd of the people of God, the New Israel.

Since the priesthood is essentially a relational reality between the priest, Christ, and through Christ to others, Fr. Dominic Maruca, S.J., asserts, "To attempt to remain faithful as a priest without a strong personal relationship with Christ is risking nothing less than emotional and spiritual suicide."[3] When the priest faithfully nourishes his relationship with Christ, he will remain strongly rooted in his identity, and, consequently will not undergo an identity crisis. In "Raising Up Priests for the New Millennium" Archbishop Dolan affirms the Christ centered identity of the priesthood with:

---

[2] Congregation for the Clergy, "Directory on the Ministry and Life of Priests, January 31, 1994," no. 2, http://www.vatican.va/roman_curia/congregations/cclergy/documents/rc_con_cclergy_doc_31011994_directory_en.html.

[3] Quoted by Archbishop Dolan in Timothy M. Dolan, "Raising Up Priests for the New Millennium," http://www.cuf.org/2003/05/raising-up-priests-for-the-new-millenium/.

Our people have no "identity crisis" about the role, mission, and ministry of priests. They love their priests; they realize that their faith does not depend on the virtue of priests but on the power of Christ; they look to their priests as messengers of meaning, who act in the person of Christ, who bring God's Word and channel the grace of the sacraments. Our laity call forth what is most noble and essential in our priesthood. While they rightly abhor clericalism, they challenge us to *priestliness*, the virtue that husbands our unique priestly identity. They call us "Father," and look to us for the love, care, and wisdom such a title implies. Our people know that priesthood is more than a job, a profession, a career, or even a ministry; they know that priesthood is a life, an identity, a permanent call that changes our very being. What I am saying is that our faithful people remind us of our *priestly identity*.[4]

In *Reclaiming Our Priestly Character*, Fr. David Toups argues that priestly perseverance and happiness are much more likely to be present when a priest understands his identity as a sacramental reality in which he participates. Quoting from a sociological study, he states:

On every measure, the priests with a cultic ecclesiology reported more happiness, less inclination to leave the priesthood, and a higher percentage saying that if they had to do it over again, they would become priests

---

[4] Timothy M. Dolan, "Raising Up Priests for the New Millennium."

again. [...In contrast] the servant-leader-type priests had lower morale and more thoughts of resigning. Our best guess is that possibly they felt a less distinctive priestly identity, providing them less self-affirmation and esteem.[5]

A priest's identity, as John Paul explained in *Pastores Dabo Vobis*, is not so much defined by what a priest does but rather by who he is; through Christ, a priest is espoused to the Church. Due to his configuration to Christ at ordination, a priest is given the opportunity to develop a uniquely intimate relationship with Christ. If he does so, he will be better able to preach the Good News, which Benedict XVI reminds us "is not a new philosophy or a new morality." Benedict XVI then adds, "We are only Christians if we encounter Christ. ... We can touch Christ's Heart and feel him touching ours. Only in this personal relationship with Christ, only in this encounter with the Risen One do we truly become Christians." Specially graced moments where we encounter Christ, Benedict XVI identifies, are "in reading Sacred Scripture, in prayer, [and] in the liturgical life of the Church."[6]

In continuity with Benedict XVI, Pope Francis affirms

---

[5] Quoted in David L. Toups, *Reclaiming Our Priestly Character* (Omaha: Institute for Priestly Formation, 2008), 122; Hoge and Wenger, *Evolving Visions of the Priesthood* (Collegeville: Liturgical Press, 2003), 124-126.

[6] Benedict XVI, "*St. Paul's 'Conversion'*, *General Audience*, September 3, 2008," http://w2.vatican.va/content/ benedict-xvi/en/audiences/2008/documents/hf_ben-xvi_aud_20080903.html.

prayer as a privileged place to encounter Christ. "The Christian life" he writes, "needs to be nourished by attentive listening to God's word and, above all, by the cultivation of a personal relationship with the Lord in Eucharistic adoration, the privileged 'place' for our encounter with God."[7] At the same time, though, Pope Francis, in accordance with the letter of James (James 2:14-26), teaches that we also are called to encounter Christ in "victim[s] of abortion, children who die of hunger or from bombings, immigrants who drown in the search for a better tomorrow, the elderly or the sick who are considered a burden, the victims of terrorism, wars, violence and drug trafficking, the environment devastated by man's predatory relationship with nature." After listing these various ways of encountering Christ, the Pope then admonishes that, "It is wrong, then, to look the other way or to remain silent."[8]

If priests do remain silent then what kind of shepherd are they? What kind of bridegroom are they? The encounter with Christ priests are called to participate in through prayer is authenticated by their effort to bring about, in an anticipatory manner, what Pope Francis calls "a culture of encounter." In this culture of encounter, through Jesus, we

---

[7] Pope Francis, "2017 World Day of Prayer for Vocations," http://en.radiovaticana.va/news/2016/11/30/2017_message_for_world_day_of_prayer_for_vocations_released/1275815.

[8] Pope Francis, "Speech of Pope Francis to the Bishops of the United States, September 23, 2015," aleteia.org, http://aleteia.org/2015/09/23/francis-to-us-bishops-speak-with-everyone-gently-and-humbly/.

form relationships that build the Body of Christ.[9] Since as a Church we collectively form the Body of Christ the Pope instructs, "We are not isolated and we are not Christians on an individual basis, each one on his or her own, no, our Christian identity is to belong! We are Christians because we belong to the Church. It is like a last name: if the first name is 'I am Christian', the last name is 'I belong to the Church'."[10] Then, while citing Benedict XVI, Pope Francis warns us against a dangerous, spiritual temptation:

> How many times did Pope Benedict "describe the Church as an ecclesial 'we'"! At times one hears someone say: "I believe in God, I believe in Jesus, but I don't care about the Church...". How many times have we heard this? And this is not good. There are those who believe they can maintain a personal, direct and immediate relationship with Jesus Christ outside the communion and the mediation of the Church. These are dangerous and harmful temptations. These are, as the great Paul VI said, absurd dichotomies.[11]

---

[9] "Creating a Culture of Encounter," wearesaltandlight.org, https://www.wearesaltandlight.org/reach-out-together/building-relationships-creating-culture-encounter-through-one-ones/; "what Pope Francis Means By a Culture of Encounter," http://cjd.org/2015/07/01/what-pope-francis-means-by-a-culture-of-encounter/.

[10] Pope Francis, "General Audience, Wednesday, 25 June, 2014," no. 1, http://w2.vatican.va/content/ francesco/en/audiences/2014/documents/papa-francesco_20140625_udienza-generale.html.

[11] Ibid.

The Cross of the Priesthood

The glorious gift of each priest to have a privileged relationship with Christ as head, as explained above by Popes, is to be expressed by service even to the extent of a priest's willingness to lay down his life for his bride the Church. Priestly service necessarily, therefore, contains a sacrificial aspect that priests are called to embrace since they are not only priests, but as Archbishop Sheen so well explained, are priest-victims. Catholic priests are priest victims because Christ, in whose priesthood they participate, was both a victim and a priest who offered himself as victim for the salvation of the world. In his words to possible future priests, Sheen said:

> The purpose of a seminary is to train priest-victims, not simply priests who offer but are not victims. In Jesus, priest and victim are inseparable. If we are not studying to be priest-victims then we are not studying for the priesthood of Jesus Christ. We are not called to be just offerors, we are called to be priest-victims.[12]

Sheen explains that priest victimhood refers to a spiritual attitude of being willing to serve and suffer for others, which does not necessarily entail doing more penitential practices.

---

[12] Bishop Sheen, *Going on Retreat*, 6 hrs and 13 mins Unabridged Audiobook, (St. Joseph Communication, 1950). This retreat was given at the Holy Trinity Seminary at the University of Dallas.

Ch. 11: Priests as Bridegrooms

In more formal language, the Congregation for the Clergy's *Directory on the Ministry and Life of Priests* similarly states that, "This sacramental identification with the Eternal High Priest specifically inserts the priest into the Trinitarian mystery and, through the mystery of Christ, into the ministerial Communion of the Church so as to serve the People of God."[13] In these few words, the Congregation defines the priesthood both in an ontological-sacramental manner and, as a consequence of the first, as a vocation of service to the People of God. These two dimensions of the priesthood are to be integrated with one another and are not intended by Jesus to be falsely separated. Unfortunately, this at times occurs, with some identifying themselves as cultic priests while depreciating the servant-leader priest model, and with others excessively identifying themselves as servant-leader priests while looking down on so-called cultic priests.[14]

---

[13] Congregation for the Clergy, "Directory on the Ministry and Life of Priests, January 31, 1994," no. 2, http://www.vatican.va/roman_curia/congregations/cclergy/documents/rc_con_cclergy_doc_31011994_directory_en.html.

[14] Joseph Ratzinger, "Congregation for the Clergy, Priesthood a Greater Love, Life and Ministry of Priests," Preliminary Reflections, http://www.clerus.org/clerus/dati/1998-12/13-6/Ratzinger_symposio.rtf.html. Pope Francis affirmed both dimensions (sacramental-ontological and service to the Church) with reference to the Church as bride and Christ as bridegroom with, "[T]he Church is Christ's – she is His bride- and all bishops in communion

Both distortions of the priesthood can set a priest up for failures in his ministry to the detriment and even abuse of Christ's flock. Two notable examples include Fr. Marcial Maciel, founder of the Legionaries of Christ, and Fr. Paul Shanley, priest of the Boston Archdiocese. On the one hand, Fr. Maciel exalted the priestly, sacramental character and went to great lengths to present himself as representing through his sacra-mental ordination his role as Father, so much so that he encouraged his followers to call him, "Nuestro Padre," that is Our Father.

After having received numerous complaints on abuse that Fr. Maciel had committed, in 2006, the Vatican stated, "since 1998, the Congregation for the Doctrine of the Faith has received accusations, which were already made public in part, against Father Marcial Maciel Degollado, founder of the Congregation of the Legionaries of Christ,

---

with the Successor of Peter, have the task and the duty of guarding her and serving her, not as masters but as servants. The Pope, in this context, is not the supreme lord but rather the supreme servant – the "servant of the servants of God"; the guarantor of the obedience and the conformity of the Church to the will of God, to the Gospel of Christ, and to the Tradition of the Church, putting aside every personal whim, despite being – by the will of Christ himself – the "supreme Pastor and Teacher of all the faithful" (Can. 749) and despite enjoying "supreme, full, immediate, and universal ordinary power in the Church" (cf. Can. 331-334)." Pope Francis, "Pope Francis Speech at the Conclusion of the Synod," News VA, Official Vatican Network, http://www.news.va/en/news/pope-francis-speech-at-the-conclusion-of-the-synod.

Ch. 11: Priests as Bridegrooms

for offenses reserved to the exclusive competency of the dicastery."[15] This was followed by a Vatican order to Fr. Maciel to live "a reserved life of prayer and penance, renouncing all public ministry."[16] Finally, in 2010, after "more than 1,000 Legionaries were interviewed, and hundreds of written testimonies were sifted through," [17] the Holy See concluded, "The very serious and objectively immoral behavior of Father Maciel, as incontrovertible evidence has confirmed, sometimes resulted in actual crimes, and manifests a life devoid of scruples and of genuine religious sentiment."[18] The pope at the time, Benedict XVI, promised Fr. Maciel's victims, "…they will not be left on their own: The Church is firmly resolved to accompany them and help them on the path of purification that awaits them. It will also mean dealing sincerely with all of those who, within and outside the Legion, were victims of sexual abuse and of the power system devised by the founder." [19]

On the opposite spectrum from Fr. Maciel stands Fr. Paul Shanley. Fr. Shanley represents a distorted version of the so-called servant-leader priest. In his role as servant-leader, Shanley became known as a "street priest" who

---

[15] "Vatican Communiqué on Legionary Founder," http://www.zenit.org/en/articles/vatican-communique-on-legionary-founder.

[16] Ibid.

[17] "Vatican Statement at Conclusion of Visit to Legionaries of Christ," http://www.zenit.org/article-29109?l=english.

[18] Ibid.

[19] Ibid.

ministered to runaway children and drug addicts. Sadly, though, he used his servant-leader role to abuse those he was helping. In 2005, Shanley, who was charged with "10 counts of child rape and six counts of indecent assault and battery,"[20] was convicted and sentenced to prison.

Reflection on celibacy as the ordinary context in the Roman Rite by which a Catholic priest becomes configured to Christ as a bridegroom can help to steer priests away from tendencies of abuse whether by using the high exalted nature of the priesthood as way to cloak abuse or by using the service dimension of the priesthood to conceal abuse. In commenting on Jesus' words, "there are eunuchs who have made themselves eunuchs for the sake of the kingdom of heaven" (Matthew 19:12 NAB), Scott Hahn explained that in ancient times eunuchs were first castrated before they were placed in charge of a king's harem. The castration of the eunuchs helped to ensure they would not abuse the king's women. Similarly, priests are called to be eunuchs, but voluntary ones. As voluntary eunuchs priests are to serve, protect, guard, and not abuse Christ's bride the Church.[21]

---

[20] "The Shanley Case," http://archive.boston.com/globe/spotlight/abuse/shanley/.

[21] Scott Hahn, *The Four Marks of the Church*, Part II, CD (Saint Joseph Communications, 1997).

Chapter 11 Discussion Questions

1. Discuss the relationship of the cultic priest model with the servant-leader priest model. Include the following in your response: sacramental, ontological, identity, Father, friendship with Christ, service to those on the margins of society, culture of encounter, the Church as we.

2. Discuss the sacrificial dimension of the priesthood. Include the following in your response: priest-victims, eunuchs, victims of priests (both by priests who are influenced more by the so-called cultic model and by priests who are more influenced by the so-called servant-leader model).

Chapter 12

Priests as Disciples of Jesus

Introduction

Pope Francis has repeatedly warned priests from becoming so overly-enamored with their office and the power associated with the priesthood that they forget to serve the People of God.[1] When this occurs, either in the direc-

---

[1] Pope Francis believes that a key way for there to be more priests who are priests because they are disciples of Christ is proper seminary formation. In addressing this issue, as represented by Aleteia, the pope provided the following principles for seminary formators to follow, "1. The formation [of future priests] is a work of art. 2. The phantasm that we have to fight is the image of religious life understood as a refuge and consolation in the face of a difficult and complex 'outside' world. 3. We have to form their hearts. Otherwise, we create little monsters. 4. And afterwards, these little monsters form the People of God. 5. We must conquer the tendency to clericalism, […] one of the causes of the People of God's 'lack of maturity and Christian freedom.' 6. If the seminary is too large, it is necessary to separate it into communities with formators who are able to truly accompany [the seminarians]. 7. Formation shouldn't be oriented only towards personal growth, but also towards its final goal: the People of God. 8. It is necessary to form people who will be witnesses to

tion of the cultic-leadership model or in the direction of the servant-leader model, priests are more likely to abuse their position of power because they have forgotten that they are priests, that they are disciples of Jesus Christ. In outlining the characteristics of a priest who serves the Church because he is a disciple of Christ, Pope Francis, as explained by Cardinal Vincent Nichols, provided "Seven 'Pillars' of Priesthood":

1) The strength of a priest depends on his relationship with Christ. … For this to happen, the priest needs to continue to grow in union with Christ through prayer and intimacy.
2) Just as he must be close to Christ so the priest must be close to the people he serves. …
3) A… priest's authority must be linked to service, especially to the care and protection of the poorest, weakest, the least important and most easily forgotten. …
4) The priest must be a minister of mercy. …
5) The priest is called to a simplicity of life. …
6) The priest must be a model of integrity. …
7) Finally the priest is to be a source of blessing for his

---

the resurrection of Jesus. 9. The formator has to keep in mind that the person in formation will be called to care for the People of God. 10. In short: we don't need to form administrators, but rather fathers, brothers, and companions on the journey." "Pope Francis's 10 Principles for Making Good Priests-No 'Little Monsters'," March 23, 2015, http://aleteia.org/2015/03/23/pope-franciss-10-principles-for-making-good-priests-no-little-monsters/.

people. [2]

This final chapter will elaborate on Pope Francis' warning against priestly clericalism and other related distortions of the priesthood by distinguishing between being a Church man and being a disciple of Christ.

Church Men

In a retreat Fr. Groeschel gave to priests, he defined Church men as "sociological figures who are identified as responsible for a particular religion. They are present to take care of the institutional aspect of religion."[3] Groeschel further explained that "Church men can be both liberal, social activists or caught up in the cultural aspect of the Church and be highly conservative people."[4] To flesh out his definition of Church men, Fr. Groeschel referred to sermon that Cardinal Newman gave titled *Obedience Without Love, As Instanced in the Character of Balaam.*

The book of Revelation describes this non-Israelite prophet of the Old Testament times as wicked. Balaam and his wickedness appears in Numbers chapter 22

---

[2] Cardinal Vincent Nichols, "Pope Francis and the Seven 'Pillars' of Priesthood," http://rcdow.org.uk/vocations/priesthood/articles/seven-pillars-of-priesthood/.

[3] The following may be correct source or it may be from another retreat Groeschel gave to priests. Benedict Groeschel, *Fr. Groeschel Speaks to Priests*, CDs (Mamaroneck: Peniel Audio & Visual Services, Inc.).

[4] Benedict Groeschel, *Fr. Groeschel Speaks to Priests*, CDs (Mamaroneck: Peniel Audio & Visual Services, Inc.).

through chapter 24. Despite being a prophet who at times obeys God, Balaam, when confronted with helping the Israelites who are traveling through the desert, disobeys God by trying to place a "stumbling block before the people of Israel, so that they would eat food sacrificed to idols and practice fornication." (Revelation: 2:14 NRSV) In his sermon Cardinal Newman first praises Balaam with:

> Balaam was, in the ordinary and commonly-received sense of the word, without straining its meaning at all, a very *conscientious* man. … [H]e was an honorable and religious man, with a great deal of what was great and noble about him; a man whom any one of us at first sight would have trusted, sought out in our difficulties, perhaps made the head of a party, and any how spoken of with great respect. …

In explaining why despite his many good qualities Balaam was displeasing in the eyes of God, Newman writes the following which Groeschel included within his definition of a Church man:

> [Balaam's] endeavor was, not to please God, but to please self without displeasing God; to pursue his own ends as far as was consistent with his duty. In a word, he did not give his heart to God, but obeyed Him, as a man may obey human law, or observe the usages of society or his country, as something external to himself, because he knows he ought to do so, from a sort of rational good sense, a conviction of its propriety,

expediency, or comfort, as the case may be."⁵

---

⁵ John Henry Newman, *Parochial and Plain Sermons*, Vol. IV, New Edition (Oxford: Rivingtons, 1868), sermon 2, 28. "[I]t will turn out that he was displeasing to God amid his many excellences.... a man divinely favored, visited, influenced, guided, protected, eminently honored, illuminated, —a man possessed of an enlightened sense of duty, and of moral and religious acquirements, educated, highminded, conscientious, honorable, firm; and yet on the side of God's enemies, personally under God's displeasure, and in the end (if we go on to that) the direct instrument of Satan, and having his portion with the unbelievers. ...

And now it is natural to ask, what is the meaning of this startling exhibition of God's ways? Is it really possible that a conscientious and religious man should be found among the enemies of God, nay, should be personally displeasing to Him, and that at the very time God was visiting him with extraordinary favor? What a mystery is this! Surely, if this be so, Revelation has added to our perplexities, not relieved them! What instruction, what profit, what correction, what doctrine is there in such portions of inspired Scripture? In answering this difficulty, I observe in the first place, that it certainly is impossible, quite impossible, that a really conscientious man should be displeasing to God; at the same time it is possible to be generally conscientious, or what the world calls honorable and high-principled, yet to be destitute of that religious fear and strictness, which God calls conscientiousness, but which the world calls superstition or narrowness of mind. And bearing this in mind, we shall, perhaps, have a solution of our perplexities concerning Balaam. ...

Balaam obeyed God from a sense of its being right to do so, but not from a desire to please Him, not from fear and love. He had other ends, aims, wishes of his own, distinct from God's will and purpose, and he would have effected these if he could. His endeavour was, not to please God, but to please self without displeasing God; to pursue his own ends as far as was consistent with his duty. In a word, he did not give his heart to God, but obeyed Him, as a man may obey human law, or observe the usages of society or his country, as something external to himself, because he knows he ought to do so, from a sort of rational good sense, a conviction of its propriety, expediency, or comfort, as the case may be. ...

Accordingly he was not content with ascertaining God's will, but he attempted to change it. ... I say plainly, and without fear of contradiction, though it is a serious thing to say, that the aim of most men esteemed conscientious and religious, or who are what is called honorable, upright men, is, to all appearance, not how to please God, but how to please themselves without displeasing Him. I say confidently, — that is, if we may judge of men in general by what we see,—that they make this world the first object in their minds, and use religion as a corrective, a restraint, upon too much attachment to the world. They think that religion is a negative thing, a sort of moderate love of the world, a moderate luxury, a moderate avarice, a moderate ambition, and a moderate selfishness. ...

Men do not take for the object towards which they act, God's will, but certain maxims, rules, or measures, right perhaps as far as they go, but defective because they admit of being subjected to certain other ultimate ends, which are not religious. Men are just, honest, upright, trustworthy; but all this not from the love and fear of God, but from a mere feeling of obligation to be so, and in subjection to certain worldly objects. And thus they are what is popularly called moral, without being religious. Such was Balaam. ... He who loves does not act from calculation or reasoning; he does not in his cool moments reflect upon or talk of what he is doing, as if it were a great sacrifice. Much less does he pride himself on it; but this is what Balaam seems to have done.

... This should be carefully considered; we are apt to act towards God and the things of God as towards a mere system, a law, a name, a religion, a principle, not as against a Person, a living, watchful, present, prompt and powerful Eye and Arm. ...

There is a right and a wrong in matters of conduct, in spite of the world; but it is the world's aim and Satan's aim to take our minds off from the indelible distinctions of things, and to fix our thoughts upon man, to make us the slaves of man, to make us dependent on his opinion, his patronage, his honor, his smiles, and his frowns. But if Scripture is to be our guide, it is quite plain that the most conscientious, religious, high-principled, honorable men (I use the words in their ordinary, not in their Scripture sense), may be on the side of evil, may be Satan's instruments in cursing, if that were possible, and at least in seducing and enfeebling the people of God. ... That is, he is thought to obey conscience, who only disobeys it when it is a praise and merit to obey it. This, alas! is the way with some of the most honorable of mere men of the world,

Disciples of Christ

In defining a disciple of Christ, in contrast with a Church man, Groeschel explained, "Discipleship is a psychological figure in the sense of being personally based. He is a friend of God, of Christ, of the Church as a mystical body of Christ, not primarily as an institution."[6] In encouraging priests to develop their relationship Groeschel said, "Jesus Christ invites one to discipleship since God is not distant but personal. ... Deepen your relationship with Jesus Christ, with God."[7]

When we deepen our relationship with Jesus in an authentic manner, Jesus naturally deepens our relationship with God the Father since, as Jesus said, "I have come down from heaven, not to do my own will but the will of

---

nay of the mass of (so called) respectable men. They never tell untruths, or break their word, or profane the Lord's day, or are dishonest in trade, or falsify their principles, or insult religion, except in very great straits or great emergencies, when driven into a corner; and then perhaps they force themselves, as Saul did when he offered sacrifice instead of Samuel;—they force themselves, and (as it were) undergo their sin as a sort of unpleasant self-denial or penance, being ashamed of it all the while, getting it over as quickly as they can, shutting their eyes and leaping blindfold, and then forgetting it, as something which is bitter to think about. ..." John Henry Newman, *Parochial and Plain Sermons*, Vol. IV, New Edition (Oxford: Rivingtons, 1868), sermon 2, 18-37.

[6] Ibid.
[7] Ibid.

Ch. 12: Priests as Disciples of Jesus

him [the Father] who sent me." (John 6:38 NRSV) Paul Vitz thinks it is important to stress the interconnectedness between developing a personal relationship with Jesus, and through the Holy Spirit, with God the Father because research of a psychiatrist colleague of his "who has worked with many members of the Catholic clergy has described the psychology of a number of priests whom he has seen…. These priests have a strong attachment to Jesus, but a weak attachment to God – especially as God the Father. They also strongly reject – some even hate – the Pope."[8]

Priests deepen their relationship with Jesus, and through Jesus with God the Father, when they heed Jesus' request to, "Take My yoke upon you and Learn from Me, for I am gentle and humble in heart, and you will find rest for your souls." (Matthew 11:29 NASB) The education to which Jesus invites priests needs to be properly understood, especially since many learned, academic priests, as Groeschel points out, "are so removed from the concept of discipleship and the reality of the living Word of God."[9]

---

[8] Paul C. Vitz, *Faith of the Fatherless: The Psychology of Atheism* (San Francisco: Ignatius Press, 2013, loc. 2071). Vitz continues with, "My colleague has said that in all these cases the psychological connection between the priests' distant and punitive father and their rejection of the Pope has been very clear. According to this psychiatrist, such a psychology is not rare even among bishops. This complex psychological interpretation, based on a split in internal father representations, remains to be fully studied and substantiated."

[9] Groeschel, *Fr. Groeschel Speaks to Priests*.

Fr. Anthony Gittins, C.S.Sp., in teaching what Jesus means in this context and others by learning distinguishes academic learning, where students gain intellectual knowledge, from apprenticeship, which is direct practical learning as an apprentice potter learns about pottery by creating pottery under the guidance of a master potter.[10] Learning from Jesus as an apprentice takes place both by developing a life of prayer,[11] which opens our eyes to rec-

---

[10] Anthony Gittins, *Discipleship*, 12 Lectures and Study Guide (Now You Know Media).

[11] In line with Archbishop Sheen, Fr. Richards in his retreats to priests encourages a daily holy hour in order to learn from Jesus. "I believe that the greatest way for a man to grow in holiness is time spent before the Blessed Sacrament. When I give retreats for priests, I always challenge them to spend a holy hour every day with Jesus in His Eucharistic Presence. I have spent a holy hour with Jesus almost every single day since I was seventeen years old, and I can proclaim firsthand that you receive great graces by being in His Presence. It is like lying out in the sun. Just by lying there you get transformed; you might not notice it, but others will. The more naked you are the more of you that gets changed. The same thing happens when you come before the Son of God! Just by being in His Presence you will be transformed, and the more open you are before Him the more you will grow in holiness! You will not notice it but others sure will! Find an adoration chapel in your city; if there is not one, then get some people together and go to your pastor and humbly ask him to start one. Commit yourself to at least one hour a week in His Presence, and if you can handle it, make that hour in the

ognize Jesus in others especially in those who are most forgotten and marginalized, as previously specified by Pope Francis, and by serving those in need. When what we do is inspired by a deep relationship with Jesus, including the necessary work maintaining the institutional reality of the Church in this present life, we will feel moved to go out of our comfort zone and evangelize.

Bishop Barron in *Catholicism* compares evangelization by the Church to Noah's ark once the ark lands on dry land. Like Noah, we are called by God to step out of the ark, out of our comfort to bring God's order into a highly chaotic world. "The ark" writes Barron:

> was interpreted, by both the rabbis and the Church Fathers, as a microcosm of God's good order maintained during a time of chaos, as a place where life was preserved behind carefully constructed walls during a season of death. And this is why the medieval architects endeavored to make the cathedrals look like ships. ... That microcosm of God's good order was not meant to hunker down permanently aboard the ark, but rather to flood out into the world and remake it. So the church gathers in a faithful remnant and

---

middle of the night, and watch what God will do! One last thing to help you to grow in holiness is to make sure you receive the sacrament of penance often; once a month is a good rule of thumb. As we talked about in chapter 3, you will be given grace through this sacrament to leave sin behind, and to forge ahead in holiness! If you do these things God will make you one of His saints!" Larry Richards, *Be a Man!* (San Francisco, Ignatius Press, 2009), 162-163.

shapes them according to God's mind, but then it purposely scatters them abroad like seeds on fertile ground.[12]

In his talk entitled "Priest, Prophet and King," Barron further explains that like Adam we have the vocation to "Edenize," meaning to remake the entire world into a garden of paradise. Adam failed since he sinned. Despite Adam's failure, we, through Christ the New Adam, are "to cultivate a garden of life in this world. We first begin doing so [this applies specifically to priests] by ordering the entire cosmos around worship, around the Eucharist. Radiating out of this Church is a spiritual energy reordering the cosmos around Christ."[13]

In the work of evangelization, it is imperative for priests and those who collaborate with them to remember that, as Pope Francis was previously quoted, "We are not isolated and we are not Christians on an individual basis, each one on his or her own, no, our Christian identity is to belong! We are Christians because we belong to the Church. It is like a last name: if the first name is 'I am Christian', the last name is 'I belong to the Church'."[14] As applied to evangelization this means, explains Vonier,

---

[12] Robert Barron, *Catholicism: A Journey to the Heart of the Faith* (New York: Image Books, 2011), loc. 2067.

[13] Robert Barron, *Priest, Prophet and King*, 2 DVDs (Spirit Juice Studios, 2014).

[14] Pope Francis, "General Audience, Wednesday, 25 June, 2014," no. 1, http://w2.vatican.va/content/ francesco/en/audiences/2014/documents/papa-francesco_20140625_udienza-generale.html.

"The Church progresses as a conquering power, not as one which goes forth to capture individual souls; the salvation of souls is a very definite kind of work, for it is salvation through the Church: let the Church be established and souls will be saved."[15]

Catholic communities priests help to establish are to evangelize by their witness to a social order inspired by the Kingdom of Heaven to come and experience in a tangible way through the Eucharist communities which allow themselves to be ordered by Eucharistic life. Those who

---

[15] Dom Anscar Vonier, *The Spirit and the Bride* (Assumption Press, 2013), loc. 2505. "If we read the Acts of the Apostles carefully we shall certainly gain the impression that apostolic activity was essentially directed to the foundation of churches everywhere, of Christian communities, with the full hierarchy, with the complete working of a spiritual system. The conquest of the individual soul seems to be subordinate to the vaster scheme of establishing the Church; it would be a very incomplete concept of Catholic activity in the mission fields to think only of the salvation of individuals: such is not directly our work as missionaries. The establishment and the building up of the Church is our work. We know how in practice, through the centuries, the missionary enterprises of the Church have had that characteristic of expanding a spiritual empire from a center, with the whole apparatus of a supernatural administration. The Church progresses as a conquering power, not as one which goes forth to capture individual souls; the salvation of souls is a very definite kind of work, for it is salvation through the Church: let the Church be established and souls will be saved."

have no faith may "come into the Church," Vonier explains, "actually, as a converted believer, or unconsciously, as one who is purified through influences whose origin he does not know."[16] Every time a mass is celebrated by the Church, may the priest celebrant and the congregation recapture the understanding of the dismissal as a calling to extend the mass throughout the day by praying for unbelievers to at least unconsciously accept Jesus Christ. In addition, may they actively witness and evangelize to a new life, a life in Christ.[17]

Chapter 12 Discussion Questions

1. After reflecting on Pope Francis' "Seven 'Pillars' of Priesthood," comment on how each pillar can be expressed in practical ways.

2. Discuss the relationship between Church men and disciples of Christ. Include the following in your response: institution, doing the right deed for the wrong reason which is "the greatest treason",[18] mys-

---

[16] Vonier, *The Spirit and the Bride,* loc. 2476.

[17] Scott Hahn, *How to Make Sense Out of the Mass,* CD (St. Joseph Communications, 2005). "*Ita Missa Est* – was understood in the middle ages not only as a dismissal but as a commission to extend the mass throughout the day to evangelize etc. In the Eucharist we are transmitted grace and then commissioned to evangelize with *ita missa est.*"

[18] T.S. Eliot, *Murder in the Cathedral* (Orlando: Harcourt Brace & Company, 1963), 44. "The last temptation is the

tical body of Christ, Bridegroom, friendship with Jesus and love of the Father, apprenticeship, evangelization, Christian community witness.

---

greatest treason. To do the right deed for the wrong reason."

www.ingramcontent.com/pod-product-compliance
Lightning Source LLC
Chambersburg PA
CBHW071115160426
43196CB00013B/2578